THE QUALITY OF LEICESTER

Front cover: *Cultural Quarter, Leicester*

Back cover detail photographs: *the Guildhall stained glass window, Turkey Café corbel, former Turkish baths, detail of banking hall window at ISKCON.*

Designed and produced by Leicester City Council.

First published in 1993 by Leicester City Council. Revised second edition published in 1997.
This third version published in 2016.

978-0-9569221-2-0 The Quality of Leicester

THE QUALITY OF LEICESTER

A journey through 2000 years of history and architecture

The former NatWest Bank

CONTENTS

Leicester Hebrew Congregation Synagogue

ACKNOWLEDGEMENTS

The production of *The Quality of Leicester* would not have been possible without the participation and assistance of so many people whose names cannot all be listed here. Their contributions are sincerely appreciated and acknowledged.

In particular, we would like to extend our gratitude to Annie Provan, Marie Hill and Stephen Nelson for all their hard work in the production of this beautiful book.

We also wish to thank photographers Ian Davis, Kerem Cetindamar, Martine Hamilton-Knight, Colin Hyde, Matt Short, Beth Walsh, David Harris, Alex Hannam, Sarah Salotti, Jeremy Crooks and Richard Kelly whose wonderful images capture Leicester's character displayed in streets, spaces and buildings, and enrich the book. Thanks also to photographers Will Johnston and Chris Gordon, Leicester Cathedral Quarter Partnership and Leicester Mercury.

Above all, we thank Michael Taylor, the author of this book, who has taken great care to bring to light many of the city's hidden architectural gems, linking the architectural development with changing demography and social history.

LEICESTER CITY COUNCIL

Aerial view of Leicester showing Clarendon Park

FOREWORD

When the first edition of *The Quality of Leicester* was published in 1993, the mood in Leicester appeared low. Our city had an important history and fine buildings but seemed to lack appreciation of its past and to have little confidence about its future.

In publishing the original volume, the city council wanted to stimulate a renewed appreciation of Leicester's rich, varied and very special character. Some 2,000 years of history have left a remarkable legacy to our city.

The first book inspired me and thousands of others. It succeeded in raising awareness of the unique value of Leicester's built environment.

In the intervening years, Leicester has rediscovered a pride in its very important role in England's history and in the impressive quality of our city.

The city of today feels very different from the Leicester of 1993. Our self-confidence has returned.

I'm delighted that this new 21st century edition of *The Quality of Leicester* captures images that will inspire fresh generations to value our historic city.

My thanks to Michael Taylor, the book's author, and all those who have contributed to delivering this new volume, including the visionary images of Leicester. My sincere thanks again to John Dean, former city planning officer, who commissioned the first edition of *The Quality of Leicester*; who inspired so many of us and to whom those who care about the quality of our city owe so much.

Peter

Sir Peter Soulsby | CITY MAYOR

The procession marking the reinterment of the remains of King Richard III, 22 March 2015

INTRODUCTION

But a city is more than a place in space.
It is a drama in time.

Patrick Geddes | 1905[1]

For a few cool, sunny days in March 2015, Leicester came face to face with its distant past. In 1485, it was the people of Leicester who were called on to witness the mutilated body of King Richard III. 530 years later, the king's mortal remains were carried through the streets and spaces of the modern city in a unique and vivid connection between past and present.

That was a special moment in the city's 2,000-year history but encounters with the evidence of the past are part of daily life. Some buildings and fragments of buildings go unnoticed while others are part of the familiar background to work, learning, leisure and travel.

Like the first *The Quality of Leicester*, published in 1993, this new book sets out to capture the essential character of Leicester's human environment as it is displayed in streets and spaces, buildings and details of buildings.

There is an intricate pattern of varied local distinctiveness across Britain shaped by geology, landscape and economy and the use of stone, clay or wood as building materials. This variety is an important part of the quality of life in Britain and the book aims to give a picture of Leicester's contribution to it. But the character of the city was not formed in some far-off time and fixed for ever; it is being made and remade every day as change is driven by a dynamic local economy and evolving social values.

Some towns may have an identity formed by a particular building stone or the use of wood in building. The mixed character of Leicester is harder to describe but there are distinct themes, like a historically small-scale approach to development and a succession of communities, which will be explored in this book.

In the years since the first *The Quality of Leicester* was published, the city has begun to face the challenges of the 21st century and to adapt to changes that were less well understood in the 1990s. Archaeology has greatly enhanced our knowledge of Leicester's distant past and our sense of living in a place that has made a really profound contribution to national history. The book can only capture snapshots but Leicester is a complex, historic city and its real character is everything that the city is and has been.

The chancel of the Church of St Mary de Castro, 12th century

SECTION ONE

ORIGINS, MEDIEVAL LEICESTER

Leicester's earliest surviving building, the Jewry Wall, established a distinct architectural character using local brick and stone. The following thousand years have left a small but prominent stock of medieval buildings in the historic town and in the villages.

Chapter one

Foundations

Close to the modern West Bridge, then (as now) a crossing point of the River Soar, a cluster of circular houses made of timber, mud and thatch was built within an enclosure in the late Iron Age: a little more than 2,000 years ago.[2] There is no evidence of the huge significance of that settlement on the ground today. But archaeology enables us to piece together a picture of what life there may have been like. In Jewry Wall Museum brooches, imported pottery and moulds for making coins suggest an ordered society with a money economy.

The first settlers were Corieltavi, a loose grouping of Iron Age tribes who settled much of the East Midlands and Warwickshire. When the Romans arrived after 43 CE the river crossing became a strategic point in the colonial road network. Ratae Corieltavorum was a significant town in Roman Britain and the tribal capital of the Corieltavi. Archaeology has given us a picture of a sophisticated town with a market hall (*macellum*), a forum, public baths and a range of houses, including elegant villas. Roman pavements and wall paintings in Jewry Wall Museum suggest a highly developed artistic sense. Between 2002 and 2009, archaeological work provided new insights into the life and buildings of the town including a collapsed section of the wall of the *macellum* in Highcross Street, houses in Vine Street, devotional objects and a lead curse tablet listing the names of 19 inhabitants of Roman Leicester.[3]

The Jewry Wall is one of the largest standing pieces of Roman building in England and is an important source of evidence about the techniques of Roman construction.[4] The wall was part of the gymnasium (*palaestra*) of the Roman baths and the two big arches connected the gymnasium to the bathing areas. In the 1930s the site was excavated before the intended building of new public swimming baths.[5] Even in this, the city's earliest surviving building, bands of long, narrow Roman bricks, granite from Charnwood, sandstone from Dane Hills and limestone from Evington begin to establish a distinctive pattern that recognisably belongs to Leicester.

Jewry Wall and St Nicholas Church

Detail of Blue Boar Lane wall painting c. 150 CE, Jewry Wall Museum

Theatrical mask from the Blue Boar Lane wall painting possibly representing the god Dionysus, Roman, Jewry Wall Museum

Peacock Pavement c. 150 CE from
Blue Boar Lane, Jewry Wall Museum

Saxon window opening on the north aisle wall (now internal) of St Nicholas Church using Roman bricks

By the fifth century CE, the power of the Roman Empire was waning and a steady transition was underway, beginning with settlement by people from modern North Germany: Angles, Saxons and Jutes. The year 410 CE saw the formal withdrawal of Roman military and officials. Change was gradual, but between the fifth and ninth centuries, a substantial Saxon settlement grew among the decaying ruins of the Roman town. Saxon Leicester was important enough to be the seat of a bishop from about the 670s and St Nicholas Church may have been the site of the first Leicester cathedral.

Roman masonry was reused in the building of St Nicholas which rose on the site of the *palaestra* in about 900 CE. Materials available on the site were used over many years in a completely pragmatic way. The tower of the church has banding in herringbone Roman brick both outside and within. Jewry Wall was incorporated as the west end of the church and this is why the wall survives today. St Nicholas Church has been much changed and expanded and the Saxon core of the church is evidenced only by fragments of masonry on the outside walls and two Saxon windows inside the nave: the only built remains of the Saxon period in the city. Roman bricks were used to form the round-arched heads to the splayed windows that, over 1,000 years ago, cast light into the nave. The tower was first built around 1100 CE and later raised. The intersecting semi-circular arches are in the Norman Romanesque style, a distinctive adaptation of classical Roman architecture often using chevrons and other bold geometrical decoration.

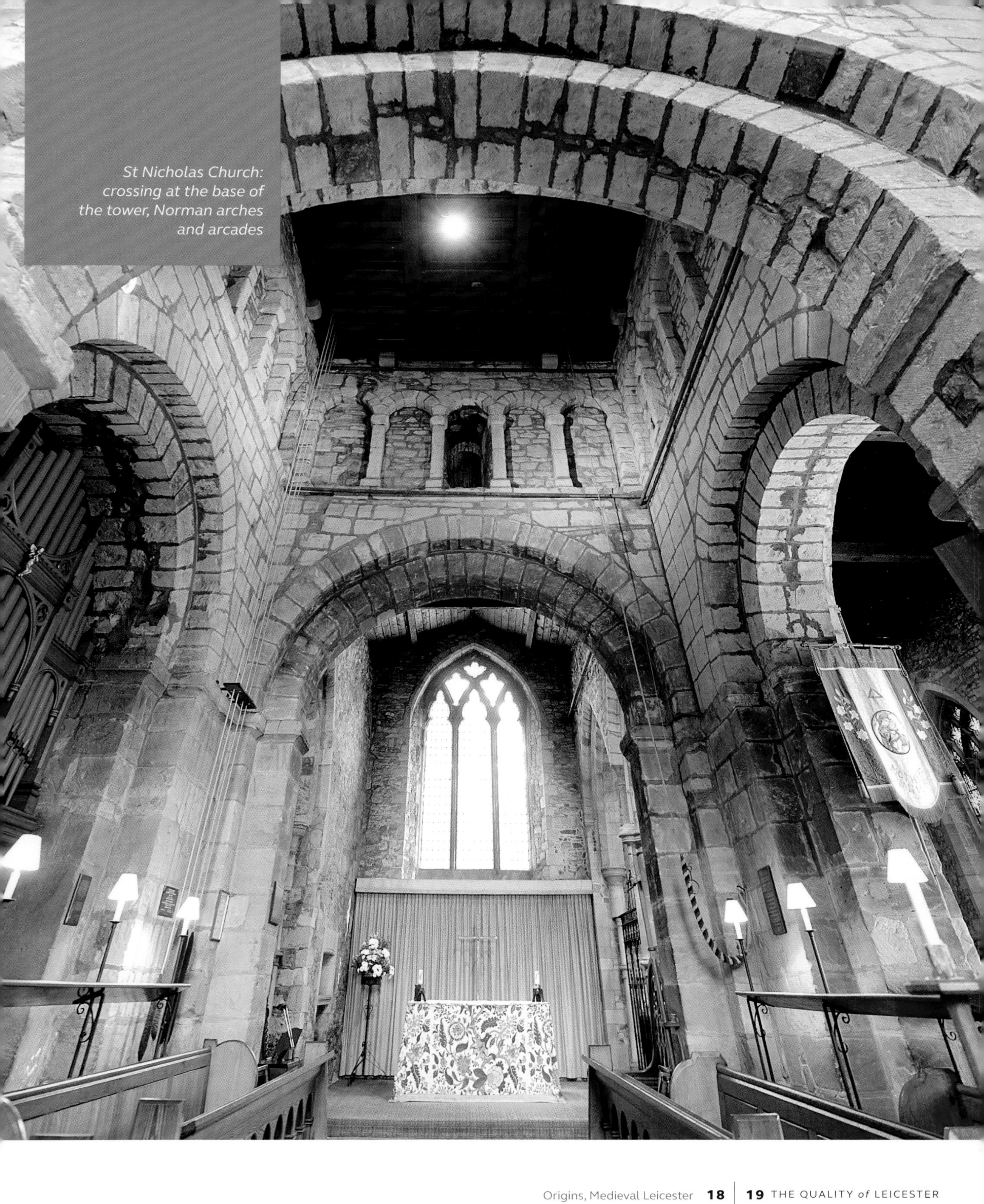

St Nicholas Church: crossing at the base of the tower, Norman arches and arcades

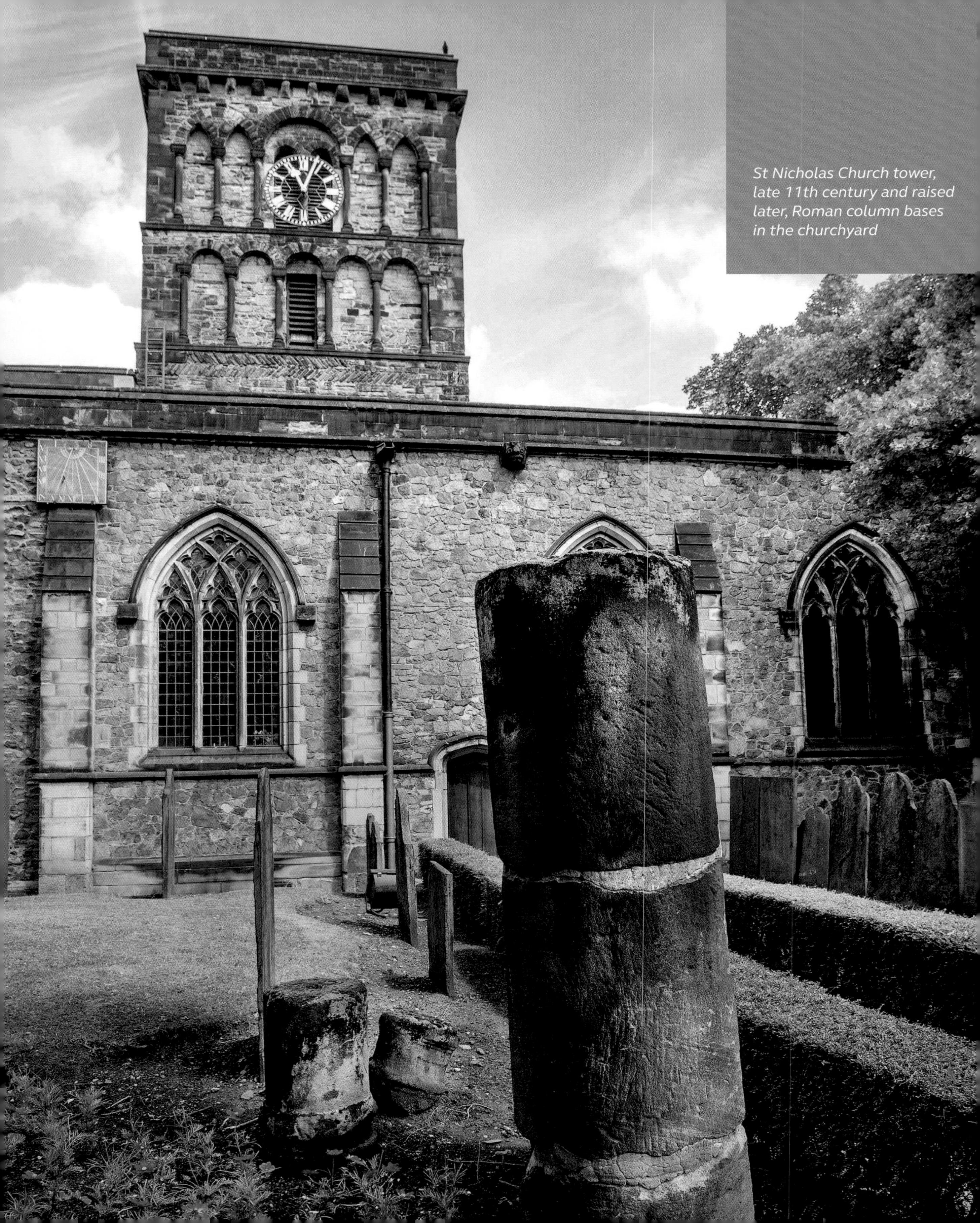

St Nicholas Church tower, late 11th century and raised later, Roman column bases in the churchyard

St Nicholas Church, viewed from Holy Bones

The era of Danish conquest and settlement in central England from early in the ninth century was a dramatic period in the city's history. Leicester was prominent as one of the five East Midland boroughs of the Danelaw but the Danish period left only street names including Sanvey Gate, Churchgate, Wood Gate, and Gallowtree Gate, from the Danish *gata* (road).

The modern city now wraps around Jewry Wall and St Nicholas. The historic buildings are seen in the context of St Nicholas Circle and the Holiday Inn, built from 1967. The elegant buildings of the former Vaughan College and Jewry Wall Museum, designed by Trevor Dannatt and built in 1960–62, frame the Jewry Wall site. Guru Nanak Gurdwara on Holy Bones reuses an industrial building to serve the religious and social life of one of Leicester's modern communities.

Jewry Wall site, Jewry Wall Museum and former Vaughan College

Chapter two

Castle and Newarke

By the beginning of the 11th century, Leicester was a relatively prosperous town. The Domesday Book records 322 houses and six churches.[6] But the arrival of the Normans in 1066 was to change Leicester profoundly and quickly. The castle, built from 1068 by the first Earl of Leicester, Hugh de Grandmesnil, was a visible symbol of a new authority in the town.

The various parts of the castle can be seen on its western flank from the river or from Castle Gardens. The defensive heart of the complex is the motte, raised by de Grandmesnil to a height of about 15 metres (reduced to make a bowling green in the 19th century), topped by a wooden stockade and surrounded by a wide ditch. After the motte came the Church of St Mary de Castro, then the Castle Hall. Together the castle and the later New Work offer the densest concentration of historic interest in the city and a complex variety of building materials and styles.

The Norman Romanesque style seen in the tower at St Nicholas continues at St Mary de Castro. This was founded by the first earl in 1107 to house a community of canons, who provided religious ministry to the castle.

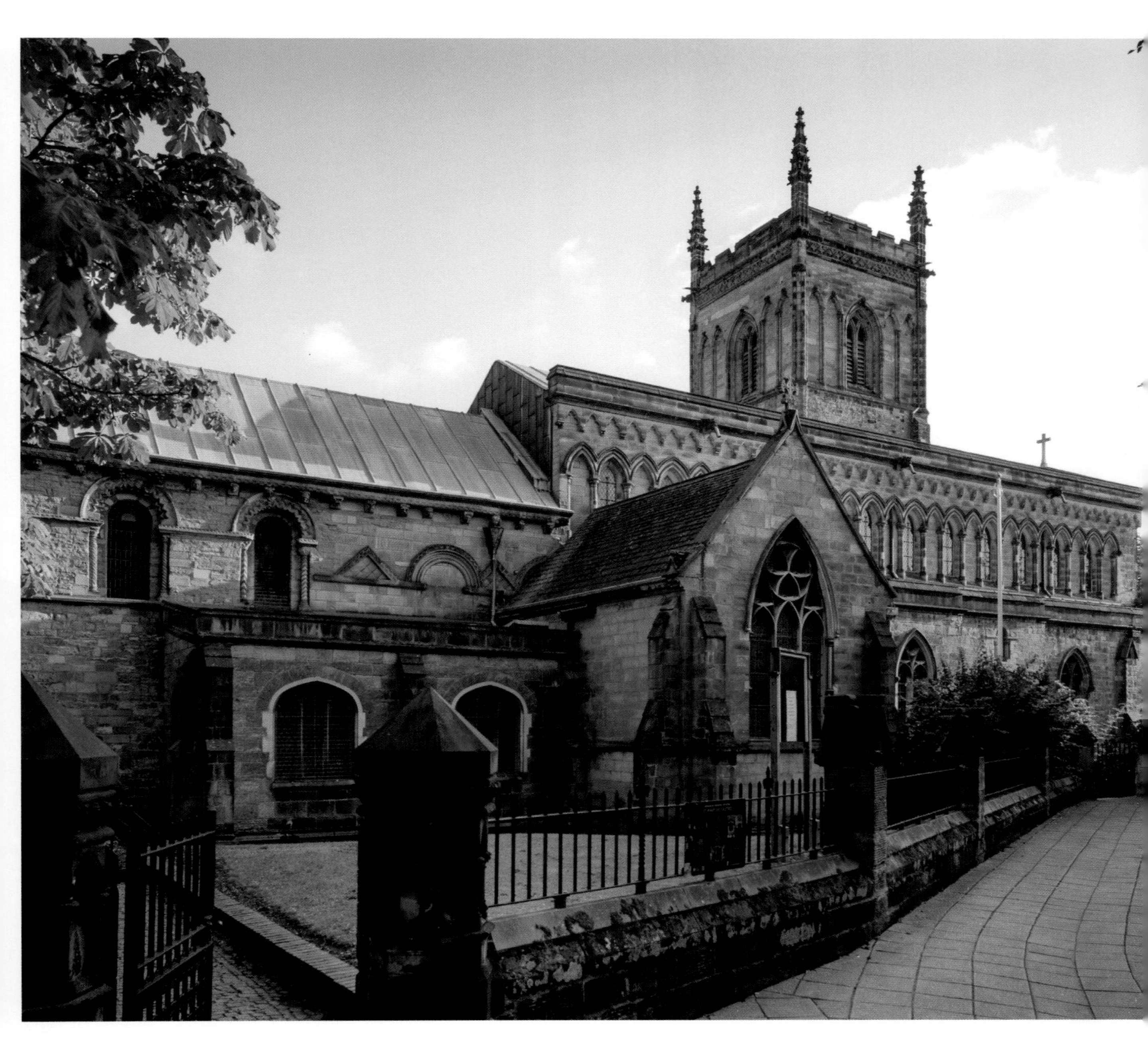

ABOVE: *Church of St Mary de Castro, from the north*
FAR LEFT: *Church of St Mary de Castro, Norman sedilia*
LEFT: *Church of St Mary de Castro tower, from the Newarke*

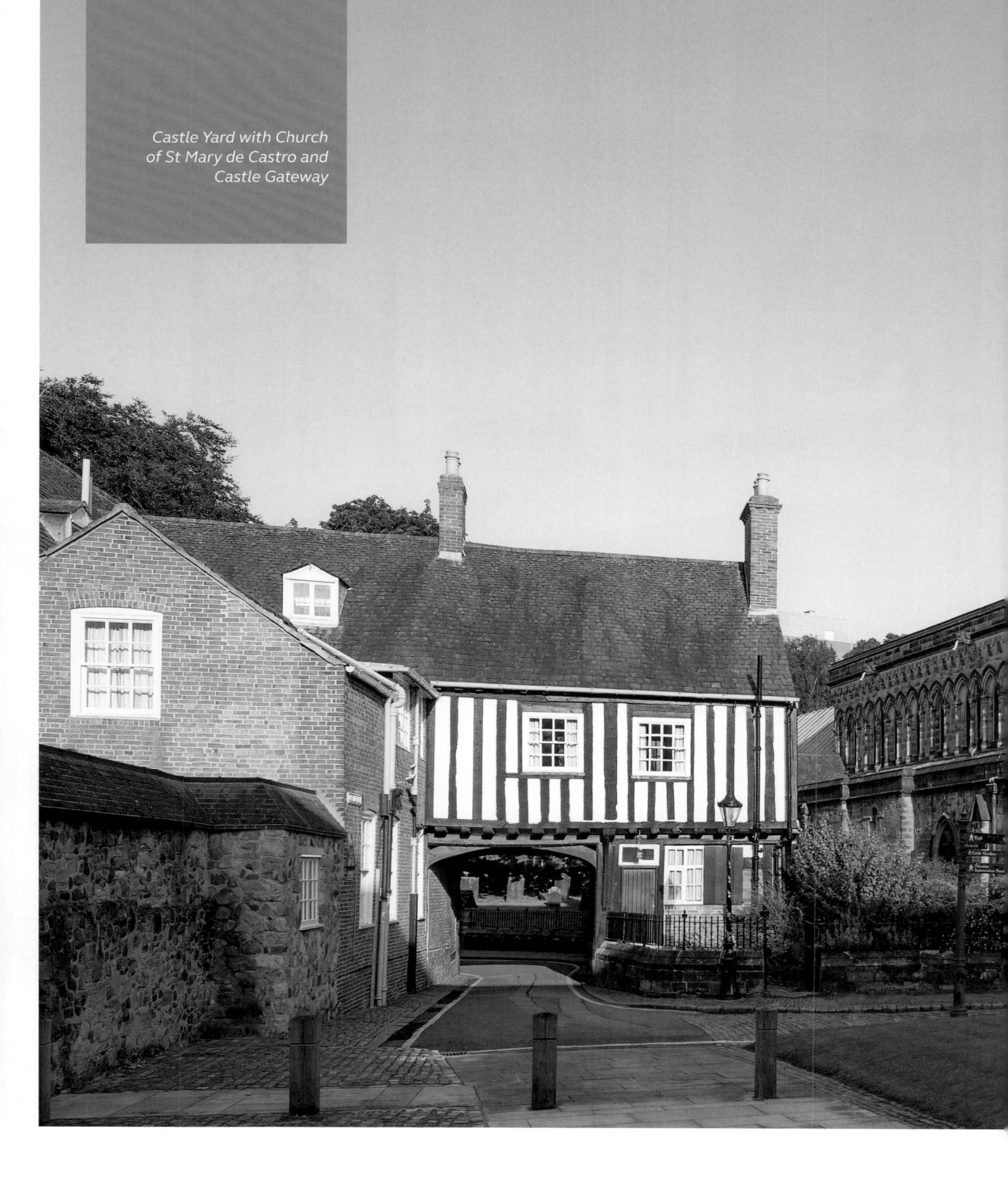

Castle Yard with Church of St Mary de Castro and Castle Gateway

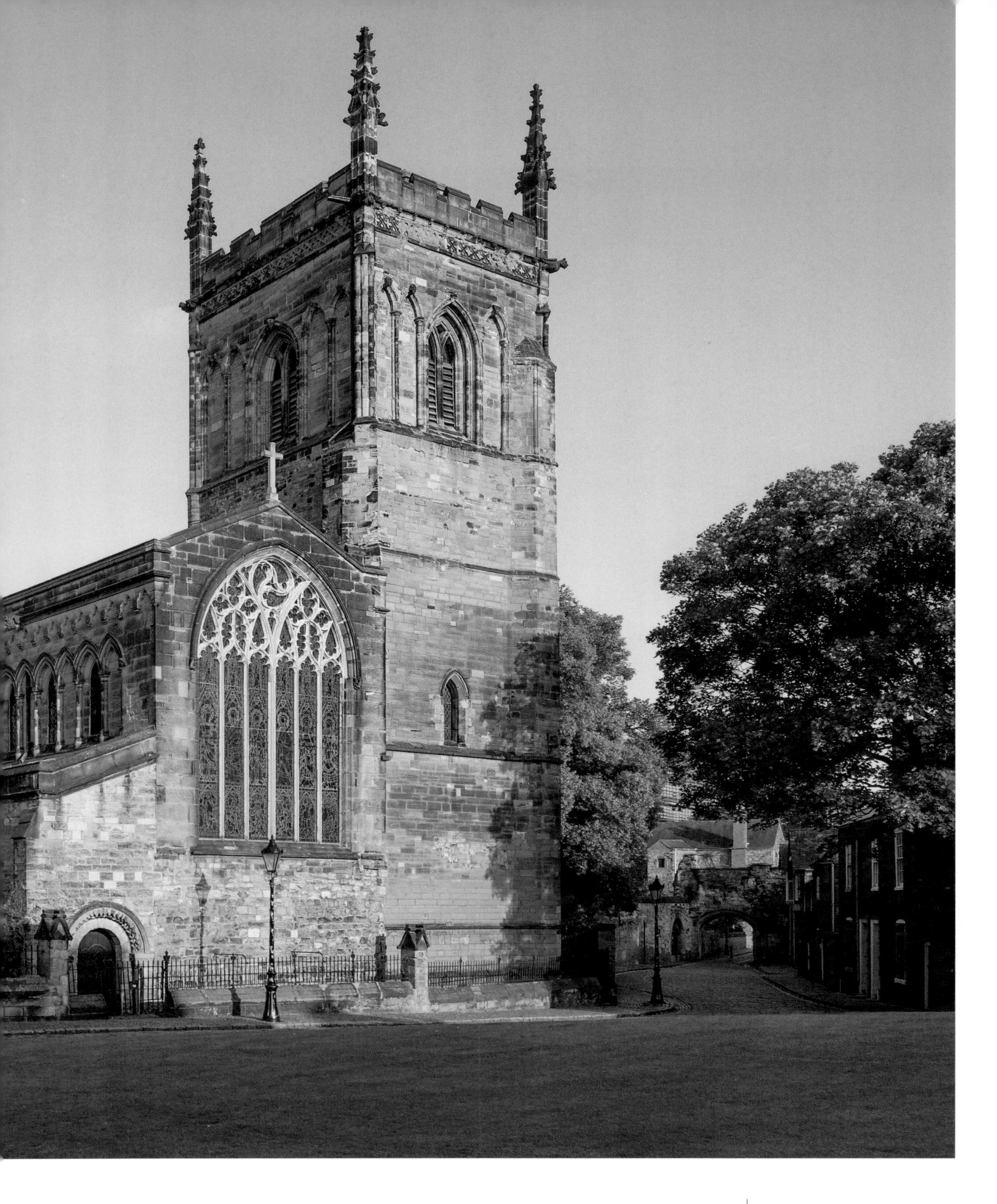

John O'Gaunt's cellar

Courtroom in southern part of Castle Hall

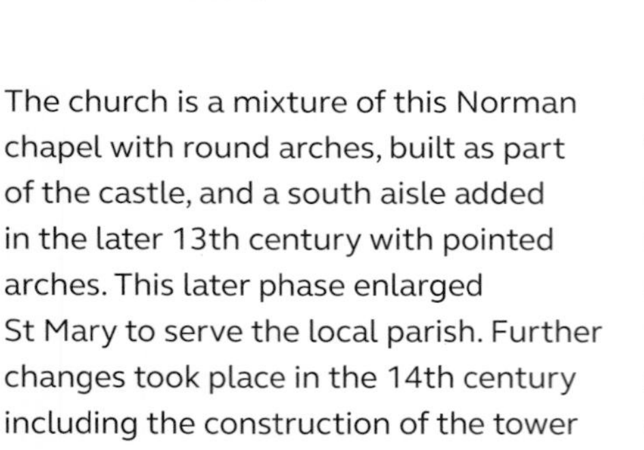

The church is a mixture of this Norman chapel with round arches, built as part of the castle, and a south aisle added in the later 13th century with pointed arches. This later phase enlarged St Mary to serve the local parish. Further changes took place in the 14th century including the construction of the tower which was imposed dramatically on the western end of the building. The Victorian restoration was carried out by Sir George Gilbert Scott, one of the most eminent of Victorian architects and a prolific church restorer. Among the treasures of the church are a Gothic sedilia in the south wall of the south chapel and an even finer Norman sedilia with round arches and zigzag mouldings. A slim needle spire built in the late 18th century was taken down in 2014 and this landmark is, for the time being, absent from the city's skyline.

About 50 years after the building of the church came the next phase: the Castle Hall. The castle was heavily damaged after de Grandmesnil's son took part

Castle Hall

in a rebellion against King Henry I and the Castle Hall was part of a rebuilding carried out by the second earl, Robert le Bossu. The Norman Hall and its timber roof, built in about the middle of the 12th century, is of national and European significance. Tree ring dating suggests that it was built in 1150-1160, giving Leicester Castle a strong claim to have the oldest domestic hall in England.[7] The hall was subdivided to provide courtrooms in the 1820s and we can now appreciate its great internal space only from historic prints. In the late 17th century, an eastern aisle was rebuilt to form the frontage to Castle Yard. This elegant addition was an early example of the post-Roman revival in the use of red brick in Leicester and thus of a building material which was to contribute perhaps more than any other to the city's architectural character.

Under an outbuilding, beyond the southern end of the Castle Hall, John O'Gaunt's cellar survives from the early years of the reign of Henry IV.

The mid-14th century Castle Gateway provides an inviting entrance to Castle Yard. The close-set timber studs (vertical members) of the storey over the archway would once have been much more typical of the architectural character of the town (see chapter 3).

Fighting took place in the castle area in 1645 when Prince Rupert's royalist army attacked the parliamentarian town. The present ruinous appearance of the Gothic Turret Gateway, built originally in the early 14th century, was the result not of these events but of an election riot in 1832. In the 13th and 14th centuries Leicester Castle enjoyed national importance as the property of the earls, later the dukes, of Lancaster, one of the most powerful families in England. It was an important centre of power in the time of John O'Gaunt, the father of King Henry IV, but became part of the royal estate and declined in relative importance after Henry became king in 1399.

The 14th century saw the development of the Newarke, an enclosed annexe to the castle containing a scattered collection of mostly religious buildings. In later centuries the Newarke became a residential area, a military drill yard and a bus station, and it is now part of the campus of De Montfort University.

The former Trinity Hospital was founded by Henry, 3rd Earl of Lancaster in 1331 and the foundation still lives on nearby. The building was much altered in the 18th century by the Derby architect Joseph Pickford and then in 1901 by R J Goodacre. Inside, the late 14th century chapel survives from what was once a much larger complex. The medieval building is still recognisable on the outside with Gothic arcades facing the Newarke, especially prominent on the north side as seen from the castle motte.

ABOVE: *Trinity Hospital, now part of De Montfort University as Trinity House*
BELOW LEFT: *Trinity Hospital* **BELOW MIDDLE:** *Encaustic floor tiles, Trinity Hospital*
BELOW RIGHT: *Trinity Hospital, east window in chapel*

The Magazine Gateway, built towards the end of the 14th century, provides a grand entrance to the Newarke from the east. The Gothic style is a later development of the style of Trinity almshouses, with flatter four-centred arches and a rib-vaulted ceiling.[8,9] The Magazine was lodging for high status visitors, but was also used to store armaments during the civil war, a use from which it takes its name. The Gateway was also a prison in the 16th century and during the Napoleonic wars. Graffiti from both eras, scratched in the soft Dane Hills sandstone, are evidence of the human misery the building has seen in its long history.

The Newarke now lends a historic dimension to the campus of De Montfort University, which overlaid it from the late 19th century. Trinity Hospital provides offices and space for events and performances, and chapter 25 will describe the new square, which reunited the Magazine Gateway and the Newarke. The Castle Hall has also been brought within the university campus. Perhaps most eloquent are the two stone Gothic arches that once formed part of the Collegiate Church of the Annunciation of the Blessed Virgin Mary, where the mutilated body of Richard III is thought to have been displayed in 1485. The arches were excavated and preserved in the basement of what is now the Hawthorn Building (see chapter 21) and form the centrepiece of the University Heritage Centre which opened in 2015.

LEFT: *Magazine Gateway, staircase* **BELOW LEFT:** *Magazine Gateway, 16th century graffiti* **BELOW RIGHT:** *Arches from the Church of the Annunciation of the Blessed Virgin Mary, now in basement of De Montfort University, Hawthorn Building* **RIGHT:** *Magazine Gateway*

19th century houses, Castle View with Turret Gateway, Church of St Mary de Castro, Wyggeston's Chantry House

LEFT: *Castle View from St Mary de Castro tower*

BELOW LEFT: *Skeffington House*

Swithland slate roof, Guildhall Lane

Leicester Castle and the Newarke contain a varied palette of building materials: local sandstone, red brick, timber, cast iron and wrought iron. The two buildings that form Newarke Houses Museum add further diversity: Skeffington House is faced in stucco and the Chantry House is built in mixed rubble stone including Charnwood slate and granite. The roof of the Church of St Mary de Castro is covered in soft-grey sheet lead. In the Magazine Gateway there are windows in late 19th century crown glass that gently distorts the view of the street outside.[10]

Some of the houses in Castle View are roofed in Swithland slate. The slate came from Swithland Woods and other sites in the Charnwood area and has a history of use going back to the Romans. Swithland slate is hard to cut to a regular size and the consequent varied gauges and thick, rugged edges give roofs a distinctive appearance. The smallest slates are laid at the ridge progressing to the biggest at the eaves. This is an important part of the distinctive pattern of building in Leicester but, although there is a second-hand market, Swithland slate has not been quarried since 1887 and it is an element of Leicester's character that will gradually be lost.[11]

Swithland slate is also a good medium for letter cutting and there are many examples on gravestones in St Mary de Castro churchyard. The slate can be incised with a crisp V-shaped cut that looks particularly beautiful in a raking light. Swithland slate can also be carved in shallow relief. In St Margaret's churchyard the tomb of the Scottish military man Andrew Lord Rollo, who died in Leicester, is a nationally notable example of 18th century slate carving (see chapter 5).[12] The slate panels give a long description of Rollo's exploits and display his arms with symbols of his military prowess.

Guildhall Lane

Chapter three

A Medieval town

Like many European towns, Leicester is shaped by a castle, the seat of aristocratic or royal power and authority, and a civic area dominated by churches, religious orders and guilds.

The medieval town developed within the walls of the Roman settlement over an area roughly bounded by the river to the west, Sanvey Gate and Soar Lane to the north, Churchgate and Gallowtree Gate to the east, and Horsefair Street and Millstone Lane to the south, linking with the Newarke at Southgates. The walls have been lost but the lines of these streets, which ran just outside them, still define the historic heart of the modern city. Suburbs such as Belgrave Gate and North Gate grew up outside the walls.

Medieval Leicester can be best understood in the area between the High Street (medieval Swine's Market) and the line of Horsefair Street and Millstone Lane. Most of the buildings in this area are much more recent but the street names Friar Lane, Loseby Lane and Cank Street (originally The Cank) remain from the Middle Ages.[13] The ma north-south route through the Roman town survives as Highcross Street and modern Applegate. The east-west route has been partly lost but the eastern section remains as Guildhall Lane and Silver Street. The layout was fashioned by changes over hundreds of years in property boundaries, adaptation to natural features and by the boundaries of the great religious houses. The main property unit, the burgage plot, had a narrow frontage to allow trading and a long plot behind for producing food, manufacturing and to provide wells and space for cess pits.

Properties were redeveloped one at a time over centuries but the shape of the burgage plot endured and the combination of an informal street layout and the rhythm of narrow-fronted plots shapes the medieval core even today.

Most of the buildings in medieval Leicester were made of wood. Many lasted into the 19th century but only a few now remain. The best of these is the Guildhall. Nearby is Wygston's House, built in about 1480. There is a 14th century cross wing at 107-109 Highcross Street and a small timber building which is now part of the St Martin's Square development (see chapter 20). Castle Gateway has been mentioned in chapter 2. The building at number nine and a few other fragments survive around the Market Place including part of what was the Angel Inn, once the finest inn in Leicester.[14]

Market Place South

Applegate

Loseby Lane, showing narrow frontages derived from burgage plots

Cank Street, originally named The Cank

Oak was the preferred material for building: it was durable, weathered beautifully and could be worked 'green' to produce gentle distortions as it seasoned, making buildings of great character and individuality. At least until the 17th century, oak was also in plentiful supply. The panels between the timbers could be filled with wooden laths supporting plaster or other materials. In the case of the Guildhall, the panels were filled with slates over which plaster was laid on wooden laths with a final covering of limewash.[15] A fragment of this type of construction survives inside Wygston's House.

The street layout is interesting and enjoyable. Walking along Silver Street from Silver Arcade to Applegate the eye is drawn along the sinuous curve of the street. The cathedral spire appears first near the centre of the view then behind buildings to the left. Approaching the junction with Loseby Lane, views open up of the turrets of the north transept of the cathedral, the spire now looming high over the street, and then of the Guildhall: a short journey that illustrates much of the history and many of the visual qualities of the medieval town.

Although parts of the medieval Church of St Martin remain in the interior, the cathedral itself is a largely Victorian building that was restored and remodelled in several phases beginning in the 1850s. Raphael Brandon was the main architect for the Victorian restoration and rebuilding, including the tall spire, now one of the city's most familiar landmarks. The grand ceremonial south porch, with statues of saints and clerics associated with Leicester, was the work of John Loughborough Pearson in the 1890s.

ABOVE: *Wygston's House*
LEFT: *Wygston's House, detail of studs with inserted slate infill and laths*
FAR LEFT: *Wygston's House*

ABOVE: *Leicester Cathedral, mid-19th century remodelling of medieval parish Church of St Martin*
UPPER RIGHT: *Leicester Cathedral, stonework detail on porch* **LOWER RIGHT:** *Leicester Cathedral, tomb of King Richard III*
FAR RIGHT: *St Martins East*

1452-1485

RIGHT: *The Guildhall, with later alterations*
BELOW RIGHT: *Guildhall courtyard with 19th century south range and late 15th century west range*

The cathedral is built in limestone and sandstone. The timber structure of the Guildhall is set on a base of Charnwood diorite.[16] The mixture of stones, timber and limewash give a glimpse of how the pattern of colours and textures in the medieval town might have looked.

The Guildhall originated as the meeting place of the Corpus Christi guild, a religious association. It was just one of a number of guilds but one that gradually attracted the wealthy and powerful elite of the town and became the focus of town government. Building took place over 200 years. First came the three cruck trusses in the Great Hall in the mid-14th century.[17] The building then developed in phases up to the later 16th century. The mayor's parlour, town library (the third oldest in England), jury room, and recorder's bedroom, show the evolving public functions of the Guildhall which was the centre for town government until 1876 when the Corporation of Leicester moved with great ceremony to the Town Hall (see chapter 11). Much of the outward appearance of the building today is the result of major restorations in 1922, when the outer coat of plaster was stripped from the timbers, and again in 1992.

ABOVE: *Great Hall of the Guildhall with three roof trusses of late 14th century* **BELOW LEFT:** *Guildhall fireplace dated 1637 in Mayor's Parlour* **BELOW MIDDLE:** *16th century coloured glass in the Guildhall's Mayor's Parlour* **BELOW RIGHT:** *Guildhall, Town library*

LEFT: *Corn Exchange* **ABOVE:** *The Market Place, first recorded 1298*

Spiritual life, town government and trade: the third surviving institution of the medieval town is the market. The present Market Place was the Saturday market, one of several in the medieval town and was referred to in borough records as early as 1298.[18] The market developed on an open area in the south-eastern corner of the town walls. One-by-one, timber structures were built against the walls and the character of the Market Place as a space bounded by buildings began to develop. As the market grew further some stalls, often those of fish and meat traders, became permanent, then evolved into shops in established buildings. This process of encroachment formed the streets and alleys between the thoroughfares named Market Place and Market Place South. The area between the back of the Corn Exchange and Hotel Street appears to have been filled in by the 16th century, forming the tapered shape of the present Market Place. The best building in this area, 9 Market Place, was built for the Corpus Christi guild in about 1500. It has prominent decorative late-Victorian or Edwardian shopfronts but its much older timber roof structure can be glimpsed through the upper-floor windows.

The Corn Exchange combined a place for trading grain to feed a growing town with a public meeting place. The architect William Flint designed a number of important buildings in the early 19th century town, including what is now the ground floor of the Corn Exchange which was opened in 1850. The upper floor, tower and bridge were added to the design of FW Ordish five years later. The two architects produced a bold Italianate building which is still the focal point of the modern market.[19]

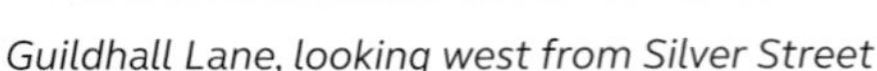
Guildhall Lane, looking west from Silver Street

Guildhall Lane

The business of buying and selling is a fundamental reason for the existence of towns throughout the world. Roman Leicester had its *macellum*. In Guildhall Lane a Norman merchant's cellar, under a building now used by BBC Radio Leicester, further illustrates the long history of the city as a place for commerce. Historically Leicester's Market Place had special areas for selling a motley range of goods: in the 16th century there was a great elm tree where women sold pigeons. It must have made a colourful and noisy scene, then (as now) a meeting place of town and country and for all of Leicester's citizens.

The redevelopment of individual burgage plots over the years produces an assorted range of building styles and materials in the medieval town. These range from Georgian Classical at 2-8 Guildhall Lane, Queen Anne style from the 1870s in Silver Street, Venetian Gothic of 1868 at the corner of Carts Lane and Guildhall Lane, and an ornate lead façade added in 1904 in St Martins East.

In 2012 a team of mainly Leicester-based archaeologists and scientists uncovered the medieval town's greatest secret. The rediscovery of the remains of King Richard III in the mundane setting of a council car park and their subsequent identification was a landmark in the city's history. The cathedral was reordered by architects van Heyningen and Hayward. The same team designed a monument of stark and moving simplicity in fossil-rich Swaledale limestone on a plinth of dark grey Kilkenny marble.[20] Leicester provided a quiet and respectful resting place for the bones of the king, half a millennium after the turbulent events of the Wars of the Roses.

Silver Street: building by FJ Hames, architect of Town Hall

Chapter four

Village in the city

As Leicester expanded in the 19th and 20th centuries the ring of villages circling the town gradually became suburbs within a continuous built-up area. Knighton, Aylestone and Belgrave were brought into the Borough of Leicester in 1892 and in 1935 Evington, Humberstone and Braunstone became part of a growing city.[21] But the villages are still distinct places all mentioned in the Domesday Book so were probably founded in the Saxon period. Layout and views, architecture and building materials all create an identity that brings the country into the city, a memory of the time when villagers may have taken goods to sell at the Saturday market beside the town walls.

Knighton is centred on Knighton Hall. Oram Cottage is a timber-framed house from the 17th century. Timber for building was becoming scarcer and is used sparingly in small scantlings or sections.

Along with part of The Cradock Arms pub, Oram Cottage is one of the few buildings in the city with a thatched roof. Among the headstones in the churchyard of St Mary Magdalene is a memorial to Denzil J Jarvis who was lost at sea on 15 April 1912 in the sinking of the Titanic.[22]

Aylestone Hall

There is still a farm within the village at Aylestone, a riverside village with a collection of bridges which will be described in chapter 23. Aylestone Hall is a complex building that originated in the mid 14th century as an aisled hall and has alterations and additions from the 17th and 18th centuries. Most of the outward appearance is due to a radical restoration in the 19th century and the hall was converted to two houses at the end of the 20th century.

Oram Cottage, Knighton

The Winstanley family, landowners at Braunstone and the owners of Winstanley House, built estate cottages around an older village green and along Main Street in 1859. Both sets of houses, Cressida Place and 1-6 Main Street, were designed by the important Victorian architect William Butterfield. He used red brick and red clay roofing tiles for both sets of houses but both designs have variations in windows, porches, gables and brickwork decoration. The simple designs show a carefully calculated irregularity which is echoed by many of Butterfield's bigger buildings. Nearby is the tranquil walled garden of Winstanley House and the hall itself built in 1775 by local builder and politician William Oldham.

In the north of the city, Belgrave village is a blend of two elegant 18th century houses (see chapter 6) with a much older settlement.

ABOVE: *School and Schoolhouse, Main Street, Braunstone*
FAR LEFT: *Cressida Place, Braunstone*
LEFT: *Section of mud wall, churchyard of St Mary, Humberstone*

The Church of St Peter at Belgrave has a fine Norman doorway.

Many houses and especially boundary walls in Leicester's villages would have been built in mud even as late as the beginning of the 19th century. It was a plentiful, cheap and easily sourced material and mud buildings are still fairly common in the rural area around Leicester. Just two small fragments survive in the city: the biggest is a short length of boundary wall in the churchyard at Humberstone. If left unprotected mud will simply slump back into the earth and the mud panels at Humberstone have their original stone base but are framed with modern brick walls and protected by a tiled coping.

106 Tennis Court Drive, Humberstone

The Church of St Mary in Humberstone was founded in the 12th century, at about the same time as the Castle Hall. It was heavily restored by Raphael Brandon (see chapter 3) in 1857–58 and has pier capitals with plant patterns superbly carved in local alabaster by Samuel Barfield.[23]

Humberstone retains a sense of what the village must have been like at the beginning of the 20th century. Along the winding main street is a set of village buildings: two manor houses, a chapel, a pub and a former pub, another of Leicester's small stock of thatched timber-framed cottages, a village school from the early 20th century, and gardens at Monk's Rest, the former vicarage.

ABOVE: *Church of St Mary Humberstone: 14th century tower, heavy restoration in 1850s* **BELOW LEFT:** *East window*
BELOW MIDDLE: *Capital carved by Samuel Barfield in Humberstone alabaster* **BELOW RIGHT:** *Capital carved by Samuel Barfield in Humberstone alabaster*

St Denys Church Evington: mostly late 13th to early 14th century, with 19th century restoration and addition

St Denys Church in Evington was begun before 1300 CE. Its development can clearly be read in its architecture. The styles of English Gothic were classified into three basic types during the 19th century. The earliest phase, called Early English, was prevalent during the 13th century and is characterised by simple Y-shaped tracery seen in the west end of the south aisle at St Denys. The west window of the north aisle is a superb example of the next phase, Decorated, which spans most of the 14th century. The tracery in this window is much more elaborate with a flowing net-like pattern enhanced by carved ornaments called ballflowers.[24] The sequence is completed by the east window of the north aisle which is an example of Perpendicular Gothic which developed from the late 14th into the early 16th centuries. In this window the bars span from top to bottom and form a square grid of tracery, in this case containing a few pieces of re-set medieval glass.

St Denys was restored in 1867 by Goddard and Paget, who added a chancel west window in a hybrid Victorian style combining elements of Early English and Decorated.

St Denys Church, Evington, interior and windows

Evington's separate identity in the early 20th century is emphasised by a village war memorial designed by Stockdale Harrison and Sons based on the High Cross (see chapter 25). The small Gothic Baptist Chapel of 1837also stands beside the village green within a setting that retains a clear sense of its rural past.

The medieval history of Evington is visible in the modern village landscape. The moated platform to the west of St Denys Church was once the site of the manor house of John de Grey, built in the 12th century. The terrain is still evocative of a vanished way of life: the remains of fishponds and a mill dam in Evington Arboretum and the long humps of a well-defined pattern of ridge and furrow on the Leicestershire Golf Club course show the ways in which the people of the manor and the village sustained themselves. The shadow of an even older landscape crosses the golf course where a footpath continues the route of the Roman road that extended the line of New Walk and Evington Footpath towards the junction of Shady Lane and Gartree Road.[25] From St Denys churchyard the view over Shady Lane across the parkland of Stoughton Grange provides a connection with a wider landscape: the rolling countryside of East Leicestershire punctuated every few miles by little stone towers and spires.

Evington village War Memorial

Site of the De Grey Manor House

Evington Baptist Chapel

Evington Baptist Chapel, detail of turrets and crenellation, windows and main doorway

New Walk

SECTION **TWO**

TUDOR TO GEORGIAN LEICESTER

The end of the medieval era brought accelerating social and economic change. The development of Leicester as an industrial city began. A substantially red brick town developed in the 18th century and New Walk was laid out south of the town.

FAR LEFT: *St Margarets Church: 13th and 15th century with 19th century restoration and addition, nave and chancel*

LEFT TOP: *St Margarets Churchyard: tomb of Andrew Lord Rollo*

LEFT CENTRE: *Tomb of Andrew Lord Rollo: detail of relief carving in Swithland slate*

LEFT BOTTOM: *Tomb of Andrew Lord Rollo: detail of Swithland slate relief carving*

Chapter five

The Tudor and Stuart transition

St Margarets Church, though built on an earlier foundation, owes its outward appearance largely to work carried out in the mid-15th century and later to Victorian restoration. At the time of the Battle of Bosworth, the stonework would have looked crisp and new. Built evidence of the two unsettled centuries that followed 1485 is scarce but some of the fragments that remain give important pointers to the later development of the city's architectural character.

Leicester can claim to have witnessed the beginning of the Tudor epoch as the new King Henry VII rode into the town after Bosworth. Among the onlookers may have been William Wyggeston, in relative terms one of the richest people ever to have lived in Leicester.[26] Wyggeston made his fortune selling wool through the staple at Calais, of which he was mayor four times.[27] His name lives on through the hospital almshouses that he founded in 1513 (now in Hinckley Road), and through Wyggeston's schools, both supported by income from the estates that he amassed.

Wyggeston endowed the Chantry House in the Newarke to house priests employed to pray for his soul at the nearby Church of the Annunciation (see chapter 2). The Chantry House was heavily damaged in the Second World War and restored in a loosely interpreted 16th century style.

ABOVE AND LEFT: *St Margarets Church: 13th and 15th century, with 19th century restoration and addition*

ABOVE: *Slab marking notional site of grave of Cardinal Thomas Wolsey*
MIDDLE: *Abbot Penny's Wall, statue niche*
FAR RIGHT: *Ruins of Leicester Abbey*

Leicester Abbey, the Augustinian Abbey of St Mary of the Meadows, was magnificent.[28] The church alone was 42 metres long and nine metres wide and reported to have been nearly as high as Westminster Abbey.[29] The foundation was wealthy and the buildings would have been richly decorated. Leicester was once again drawn into national history in November 1530 as Cardinal Wolsey, one of the most powerful figures in Tudor England, died and was buried there on his way to London to be tried for treason. After its dissolution in 1538, the treasures of the abbey were dispersed and saleable building materials quarried for reuse. What remains today in Abbey Park is an interpretation of the layout marked by low stone walls following archaeological excavation in the 1920s.

Around the Abbey grounds, the precinct walls also remain. Abbot John Penny left Leicester in about 1500, so the brick section of the walls that bears his name running along Abbey Lane must have been built in or just before that year. Blue brick patterns in the wall display Penny's 'JP' initials, a chalice, crosses, sacred monograms and abstract patterns.[30]

INFIRMARY AND GUEST HALL

Abbot Penny's Wall, Abbey Lane: detail of JPc initials (John Penny construxit)

Brick fell out of use in England after the Roman period but was reintroduced into Leicestershire in the late 15th century. In the 1480s, a mason from Flanders was employed at Kirby Muxloe Castle to make and lay bricks and local masons were sent to Tattershall Castle in Lincolnshire to learn the craft of brick building.[31]

Mud and timber were easily available and brick was at first a high-status material, reflected in its use for the frontage building to the Castle Hall in 1695 (see chapter 2). There must have been other brick structures in the Tudor town but, after the Roman period, Abbot Penny's Wall is the earliest surviving use of a material which was to become Leicester's signature.[32]

The 16th century saw advances in education, funded by charity as a civic benefit. The Free Grammar School in Highcross Street has been much changed and often neglected. It was built from materials salvaged from the nearby medieval Church of St Peter, including tie beams with bosses and ornamentation.[33] The outer walls are in salvaged limestone, sandstone and granite laid as rubble. A plaque on the wall of the Free Grammar School records a contribution to the cost of founding the school of £10 from Queen Elizabeth I and, listed second, from William Wyggeston who left £20 in his will.[34,35] The building has been subject to several programmes of restoration, not all of which would now be regarded as appropriate. The most recent was carried out as part of the development of Highcross shopping centre within which the Free Grammar School is now the 1576 Restaurant.

The guilds were dissolved in 1547 and in 1563 the Guildhall (see chapter 3) was formally conveyed to the corporation. The mayor's parlour was formed in the western range in 1637 including the addition of a magnificent carved overmantel to the fireplace. In 1632 the town library was moved to the eastern range of the Guildhall from St Martins Church. The growing confidence of civic government was reinforced in 1587 when Queen Elizabeth I granted Leicester its first charter of incorporation, enabling the corporation to own property for the first time and to receive the rents from the weekday market.[36]

Timber roof structure inside the former Free Grammar School, now a restaurant

Free Grammar School

The English Civil War hit Leicester hard. The town's sympathies were generally Parliamentarian, though the corporation had tried to stay out of the war. But Leicester was attacked by the king's army in May 1645, shortly before the decisive defeat of the Royalist army at Naseby about 20 miles to the south. There was heavy fighting culminating in the sacking of Leicester by the king's forces and extensive damage to lives and property.[37]

The most evocative memorial to the Civil War in Leicester is the gaunt stone ruin of Cavendish House in Abbey Park. Built in the early 17th century by the Countess of Devonshire on the site of the abbey gatehouse, the house served as a lodging for Royalist forces during the Civil War. After the defeat at Naseby, Cavendish House was sacked and burned leaving the smoke-blackened shell that remains in Abbey Park today, preserved as a ruin for 350 years of its 400-year life.

Aside from the drama of national events, a quieter change took place in Leicester which was to transform the medieval market town into an industrial city. Writing in 1815, the Leicestershire historian John Nichols recorded:

[in 1680] Alsop, a Northamptonshire man, came to Leicester and resided in the Parish of All Saints at or near the North gateway, where he followed the occupation of stocking maker, being the only person in that trade In Leicester.[38]

Medieval Leicester had industry of sorts, especially trades based on wool. But stocking-making became the town's main industry and the driving force for change and growth over the next two centuries.

Ruins of Cavendish House

LEFT AND FAR LEFT:
21 St Martins, doorway
21 St Martins

Chapter six

Belgrave and the Georgian town

The transition from the proportions of a classical column in Rome, or those of the columns in St Nicholas churchyard, to the design of a Georgian house is a long and complex story involving architects and scholars in the Italian Renaissance and architectural visitors from Britain to Italy and France. The result is a system of proportions which, with variations, give Georgian houses much of their consistency, expressed (for example) in the progression of window sizes in which the tallest are often on the first floor and the smallest at the top.

After a slow beginning (see chapter 5) the use of red brick in Leicester became established in the 18th century. This is the other factor that gives the Georgian town so much of its character and harmony. Brick was durable, easy to produce in volume and the raw material could be found close at hand. Leicester was marked by numerous brick-clay pits into the early 20th century. Their products came in a range of colours from the brownish reds of Belgrave Hall or 17 Friar Lane, to the orange-reds of the typical Victorian terrace and even to a whitish brick. The colour of red brick is determined by the proportion of iron in the clay; lime-rich clay produces a white brick. Where they were directly exposed to the flame in the kiln, bricks could acquire a hard, glass-like surface, often of a darker colour, which could be exploited to make decorative patterns.[39]

The architectural style of Georgian Leicester began to develop before King George I came to the throne in 1714. The earliest surviving complete, free-standing brick building in Leicester is the Great Meeting Unitarian Chapel in East Bond Street, built in 1708.
It has a pared-down classical style with a little decoration of blue and white of bricks. The chapel is a landmark in the city's architectural development and historically significant for its many connections with Leicester's civic history. It also forms the centrepiece of an intriguing group of buildings including the Gothic church school building of 1859, now attached to the chapel by a modern glazed infill building, a boundary wall in brick and a variety of sandstone, slate and igneous stones from Charnwood, and a four-storey timber warehouse of about 1830.

ABOVE AND LEFT:
Great Meeting Unitarian Chapel, East Bond Street

ABOVE: *Belgrave Hall stables* **ABOVE MIDDLE RIGHT:** *Belgrave Hall, front door* **ABOVE FAR RIGHT:** *Belgrave Hall, elevation to garden* **BOTTOM RIGHT:** *Belgrave Hall garden* **BOTTOM FAR RIGHT:** *Belgrave Hall, entrance hall*

Belgrave contains an exceptional group of Georgian buildings and spaces. Belgrave Hall is a comfortable and plain family house built from 1709 (the earliest of various dates shown on the rainwater heads) by Edmund Cradock. The front elevation, to Church Road, is quite restrained with a parapet providing a flat skyline. The simplicity of form is relieved by detail and patterning: the regularly-spaced dark purple headers in the brickwork, and railings and a gateway in wrought iron worked by the blacksmith into delicate leaves and spirals.[40]

The lead rainwater heads are especially good with bold applied initials and arms of the Cradock family. Today the leadwork at Belgrave Hall is maintained by the Leicester company Norman and Underwood Ltd, who are also important producers of sand-cast lead sheet, especially for the roofs of churches and cathedrals, cast by a method little changed since the time of the Romans.[41]

The Cradocks sold Belgrave Hall to the Vann family shortly after its completion. The property then passed to John Ellis and eventually became a museum in 1936.[42] Barley-twist balusters on the main staircase, each one slightly different, and the gently worn stone paving in the hallway evoke the lives of the people who made Belgrave Hall and have used it over 300 years.[43]

Left to right: Belgrave Hall, Belgrave House, St Peters Church, Belgrave House Stables

FAR LEFT: *Belgrave garden gate pier*
LEFT: *Belgrave Hall garden*
RIGHT: *Belgrave House*

The garden, little changed from its late-Victorian layout, has been a place of rest and delight through the centuries, as it is now. The Holdsworth Cenotaph (Edward Holdsworth b. 1684), sculpted in Carrara marble by Richard Hayward, was brought from Gopsall Hall in 1951 as part of the museum display.[44, 45] The sculptures form focal points among a fine collection of trees, including a venerable mulberry.

Belgrave House overlooks the garden from across Church Road. It was built in 1776 for William Vann as a more elaborate classical composition than the older building nearby tall arched central bay, stone string courses and single-storey flanking wings with stone balustrades.[46] In a further contrast with Belgrave Hall, the brick is a lighter orange-red and of a larger size than the bricks on the earlier house.

Belgrave House and its stable block were converted to flats by developer Naresh Parmar and architect Brian Dearlove in 2011–12, opening a new phase on the 250-year life of the buildings.

LEFT: *New Street, dog-leg bend, looking south*
TOP RIGHT: *11 New Street, doorway*
BOTTOM RIGHT: *10A New Street*

In the city centre, the main concentration of Georgian houses and streets was built on the site of the Greyfriars friary between Peacock Lane/St Martins and Millstone Lane. Only a fragment of wall from the priory remains above ground in a car park to the west of New Street. The estate had passed through various ownerships before being sold to Thomas Noble in 1711 and then passed to Rogers Ruding in Noble's will. New Street was laid out by about 1750 and parcels of land then sold for development.[47] The bend in New Street may have followed a boundary or a natural feature and the overall layout of the Georgian town is informal and small scale rather than an echo of the elegant streets and squares of Georgian Bath or Edinburgh.

Whatever the reason for the shape and narrow width of New Street, they produce some of the best street views in the city. The splayed side bays of numbers 12–14 act as a hinge at the bend in the street, leading the eye northwards to the cathedral tower and spire seen in a narrow slot between buildings. Looking south the big pediment of 6–8 New Street, set on a diagonal, holds back the view towards Friar Lane.[48]

The interest of the Georgian town also lies in the design of individual buildings and details of buildings. Number 21 St Martins, built early in the 18th century in a thin red-brown brick, has an imposing doorcase and windows fixed flush with the outside wall. Later in the century, windows tended to be set in reveal exposing part of the thickness of the wall, partly to restrict the spread of fire across the face of the building. Because of the technical problems in producing glass at this time, Georgian windows usually had small glass panes fixed in narrow glazing bars.

Street view looking north along New Street to the Cathedral tower and spire

The Georgian town also has good examples of front doors designed to impress visitors and passers-by as the focal point of the house. The doorway at 21 St Martins has a big segmental pediment.[48, 49] Number 11 New Street has the most ambitious doorway with buff sandstone Roman Doric columns supporting a porch canopy.[50] The entrance to 27 Friar Lane has a wide fanlight over a panelled door and side panels.[51] At numbers 23–25 Friar Lane the doorcase is much plainer with a rectangular fanlight in a simple opening. Back in New Street, number 16 has a solid, square doorcase with big projecting stone brackets.

Friar Lane contains the widest variety of materials and of architectural styles,

LEFT: *27 Friar Lane, Gothic window heads* **BELOW LEFT:** *27 Friar Lane, doorway*
BELOW: *18-28 Friar Lane, 19th century terrace in white brick*

17 Friar Lane

both Georgian and later, in the area. Surface materials include white stucco at numbers 23–25 and a 19th century terrace in white brick on the south side. The highlight, and one of the best Georgian buildings in the city, is number 17 Friar Lane, built between 1759 and 1771 for businessman William Bentley.[52] It was designed to be noticed, combining a selection of Georgian architectural motifs including a deep pedimented door case, a Venetian window, a Diocletian window and rusticated limestone pilasters.[53]

Behind a plain frontage in Friar Lane are the remains of a Turkish baths, rebuilt in 1872 to the design of architect and engineer John Breedon Everard. Advertised at the time as "equal to any in the provinces", the remaining room contains red granite columns with capitals carved in the style of Samuel Barfield, including plant and bird motifs and even a lizard.[54] The columns support intersecting Gothic arches that carry a lofty lantern whose coloured glass casts an enticingly oriental light into the room.

During the 20th century, the Georgian town became a favoured location for small professional and business offices, but this use had declined by 2000. Despite some revival of housing in the area it stood in need of investment. In 2015 Leicester City Council secured £1.1 million from the Heritage Lottery Fund as part of a £1.6 million scheme: the Greyfriars Townscape Heritage Initiative. This fund is intended to encourage investment from the private sector and to improve the economic prosperity of the Georgian town and protect its historic importance.

Former Leicester Trustee Savings Bank, Leicester wyvern and cinquefoil

ABOVE AND FAR LEFT:
Former Turkish Baths on Friar Lane
LEFT:
Turkish Baths on Friar Lane, details of windows, tiles and column capitals

Chapter seven

Susanna Watts's Leicester

Leicester was already a substantial industrial town by 1800, based on the growing manufacture of hosiery. One woman left us a picture of the town at the point at which change was gathering pace. Susanna Watts was strongly principled and devout, and a resolute campaigner against slavery and for the rights of women. In 1804 she published a guidebook entitled *A Walk Through Leicester*.[55] Miss Watts's writing is lucid, sharply observant, opinionated and still a delight to read. Many of the landmarks she describes have been lost but her picture of the town remains vivid. To take just one example, we can still stand in St Margarets churchyard and read the inscription on Lord Rollo's tomb from the same piece of slate that Miss Watts carefully recorded over 200 years ago.

A Walk Through Leicester was published at the bookshop of Thomas Combe in the building now known as City Rooms, which Watts describes as the first modern architectural ornament of the town.[56] City Rooms looks both solid and refined with a base in rusticated stonework, large areas of fine-grained sandstone ashlar and three big windows lighting the first-floor ballroom.[57] Statues of Music and Dancing by Rossi and Bingley (John Charles Felix Rossi and John Bingley), made in artificial stone, and relief panels of dancers in Coade Stone give movement and energy to the front of the building.[58]

RIGHT:
City Rooms, ballroom interior

T:
Rooms

OW:
tue representing ter in the ballroom ity Rooms. The ues representing seasons were gned by John Bacon Elder and made by de and Sealy

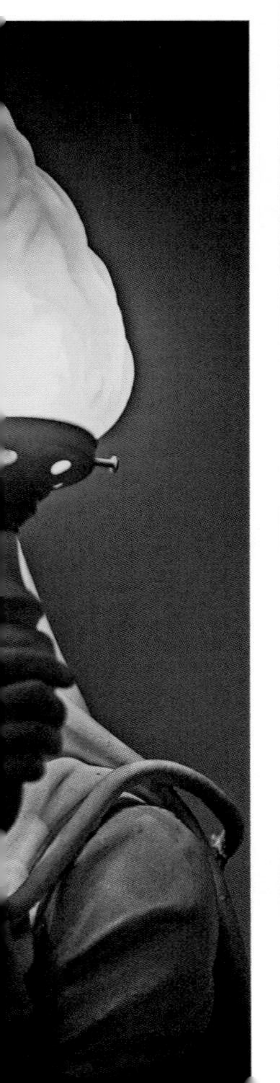

Former County Fire Offices

Former Saracen's Head

City Rooms was designed by John Johnson, a Leicester architect who made his name in London and elsewhere. Built between 1792 and 1800, the hotel never succeeded financially but was used as assembly rooms for social gatherings. The ballroom, sparingly and simply decorated, is still one of the most elegant rooms in the city. After many years of civic use, City Rooms was converted to a venue for conferences and social gatherings by Naresh Parmar and his architect Brian Dearlove in 2004–05. The ballroom again hosts stylish events and guests can stay in the rooms of the hotel.

City Rooms is at the centre of a notable group of buildings including the County Fire Offices in Market Place South built in 1817, stucco-fronted and in a style to become prevalent in nearby King Street.[59] The pub now known as Molly O'Grady's was built as The Saracen's Head in 1901 to a bold Arts and Crafts design by Stockdale Harrison and Sons. The role of women in the hosiery trade, burgeoning in Miss Watts's time, is celebrated in James Butler's 1990 bronze sculpture of The Leicester Seamstress in front of City Rooms.

Many of the guests at the hotel would have been attracted by the races to the south of the town on the site which is now Victoria Park. In 1785 a promenade was laid out linking the racecourse to the town on the line of the Roman *Via Devana* and along an important parish boundary. Initially a simple gravel path known as Queen's Walk, modern New Walk has been free of powered traffic for well over 200 years.

New Walk, junction with King Street

New Walk Museum, New Walk and Museum Square, 1836

For Miss Watts, New Walk would have been an optional diversion from her progress through the town and would have been less than 20 years old when she described it. New Walk had not been created for entirely noble motives. The powerful borough freemen owned grazing rights to the Southfields, the subject of a long dispute with the corporation, which was finally resolved in 1804 (see chapter 8). The laying out of New Walk was in part a way of establishing the corporation's claim over the land to the south.

Spaces for small parks were left as the Southfields developed in the decades after 1804, adding to the attraction of what was becoming a fashionable residential area. Museum Square is shown on a map of 1844 and De Montfort Square followed as building proceeded from the 1840s to the 1860s. The Oval appears to have been formed from a kink in the otherwise regular line of the walk as development spread southwards.[60]

Trees are critical in containing views and leading the eye through enclosed stretches of promenade and others where views of varying extent and character open up. The steady uphill gradient to the south and sinuous curves in the line of the walk cause views to be progressively held back and opened up as the walker proceeds along the route. The avenue of trees also maintains the continuity of the walk which survived the building of the railway in 1840 and of Waterloo Way in the 1970s.

The road crossings provide glimpses of landmarks such as the fire station tower and the railway station frontage. At the southern end of the walk, the lodge to Victoria Park provides an architecturally distinguished end-stop (see chapter 16). Miss Watts suggested that her imaginary visitor should climb the steps of a windmill here "at the London toll-gate" to enjoy views stretching as far as the peaks of Derbyshire.

The Oval

New Walk and the Oval railings

Susanna Watts knew the walk free of buildings and it remained so until 1818 when the Dominican friars at Holy Cross Priory built their church end-on to the walk. Building development followed and, although this was a piecemeal process by various builders, the corporation established design rules so that building was set back from the edge of the walk and the front gardens were enclosed by a wall and railings. This provides a consistency which united varying building styles. Many of the present railings were reinstated in the 1990s and 2000s as replacements for lost ones.

Classical styles in various forms dominated New Walk and continued the proportions of the Georgian town into the earlier phases of development.

Numbers 7–17, built around 1852 by Flint and Wickes (Charles Wickes b. 1828) are faced in brick with solid surrounds to windows and doors. Next to them, numbers 19–21, built a little after 1844, are faced in stucco and have slimmer surrounds to windows and doors providing a more delicate appearance. The early pair at 23–25 are even more refined with flat window surrounds and little curved bay windows on the ground floor. Opposite this group, the design of an office building of the early 1970s attempts to echo the rhythm and vertical lines of New Walk in concrete and in an idiom of its own time.

BELOW: *19-21 New Walk* **ABOVE AND BELOW MIDDLE:** *Holy Cross Priory*
BELOW RIGHT: *62-64 New Walk and Courtview, late 19th century, from Museum Square*

Facing Museum Square, on the east side of New Walk, is a group of houses that show the influence of the Greek Revival. Until the mid-18th century classical architecture in Britain was based on Roman models. Greek classical architecture was introduced to England by James 'Athenian' Stuart and Nicholas Revett, two intrepid young men who travelled to what was then part of the Ottoman Empire and published the collections of drawings they made there. The Greek style was slow to become popular but the group in New Walk had been built by 1828. Numbers 62–64 New Walk have a Greek Key frieze and small *anthemion* (honeysuckle) motifs on the capitals and in the ironwork.[61] The white terracotta chimney pots are based on Egyptian pylons.[62]

Numbers 78–80 New Walk, built around 1836, are stucco-fronted and simply detailed with delicate wrought iron balcony railings on the first floor. The Greek anthemion appears again in the pattern of the ironwork. The group provides a foil to the big portico of the museum.

To the south, development began around De Montfort Square in the 1840s. Numbers 98–104 New Walk have simple classical details in pinkish brick and stone with neat fanlights over the doors. The upper floors were built up later and some of the houses have bays, a then-fashionable addition, probably made in the 1870s, intended to add space and light to the internal rooms. The terrace by William Flint on the north side of De Montfort Square, now sheltered flats for elderly people, forms a palace front, a terrace with emphasised end and central bays making a single grand composition.

ABOVE: *Anthemion decoration in ironwork, 74-80 New Walk* **TOP LEFT:** *23-25 New Walk* **TOP MIDDLE:** *74-80 New Walk* **TOP RIGHT:** *74 New Walk, doorway and reinstated railings* **BOTTOM RIGHT:** *De Montfort Square*

Upper New Walk at junction with Granville Road

Classical styles hung on in provincial Leicester after Gothic had become fashionable in many other towns. In the 1860s the builder William Rushin developed a run of paired houses between De Montfort Street and University Road in orange-red brick and stone maintaining the established style of New Walk.

There is an abrupt change of mood south of University Road. The hill is slightly steeper and the line of the walk takes a left-hand bend. The sequence of houses on the east side of Upper New Walk was built in the 1880s in a Domestic Revival style based on historic English architecture rather than Roman or Greek precedents.

Number 2 University Road and 146–154 Upper New Walk were designed by Stockdale Harrison in red brick with clay-tile roofs. Big gables face the walk, forming a dynamic eaves line and the designs mix timber framing, a corner turret, wooden balconies, leadwork and stone.

146-152 Upper New Walk

ABOVE *154 Upper New Walk*

LEFT: *2 University Road*

New Walk Museum, 1836

New Walk, looking north from University Road

Residential or former residential buildings provide the linking elements to the architecture of New Walk but landmarks provide features that draw the eye and form a memorable image of the walk.

At the northern end Holy Cross Priory church, Perpendicular Gothic but a relatively modern building, is an imposing presence on New Walk. Further south, the grand entrance of the museum stands back in a small space of its own. The building began life as the Nonconformist Proprietary School in 1836. Its architect, Joseph Aloysius Hansom also designed the Baptist 'Pork Pie' Chapel in Belvoir Street (see chapter 11) and, further afield, the classical masterpiece of Birmingham Town Hall and several notable Roman Catholic churches in Gothic style.

The entrance to the museum is through four great columns in the Tuscan order (a type of Roman Doric) and show

New Walk looking south from the Oval with St Stephens Church

marked enstasis.[63] The severe simplicity of the great portico echoes the seriousness of purpose of the educators who built the school and the founders of the museum which have used the building since 1849.[64]

The slim spire of St Stephens United Reformed Church, at the junction of New Walk with De Montfort Street, rises elegantly above the trees. ARG Fenning designed the church for a site next to the train station on London Road. In the 1890s, when the present entrance to the station was built, the church was moved to its present site. It was rebuilt a bay shorter and there was enough of the light brown limestone left over for the front of the manse next door.

University of Leicester, School of Museum Studies

Not all the 20th and 21st century additions to New Walk have been equally successful in adding positive quality to it. But a detached house at 155 Upper New Walk fits quietly and modestly into the scale and urban form of the walk. The former School of Education (now the University of Leicester, School of Museum Studies), designed by Douglas Smith Stimson Partnership and opened in 1966, still looks bright and modern, especially when glimpsed through the trees around the Oval.

At the far northern end of New Walk, new commercial and residential buildings on the site of the former New Walk Centre promise to provide new landmarks and a public space. These will continue a long process of building and rebuilding and reinforce the quality of the walk as a continuous urban open space.

Lamp columns and arches contribute to the relaxed use of New Walk and add detailed visual texture and a running theme that unites diverse spaces and vistas. The arches at King Street, Waterloo Way and De Montfort Street have a lotus-leaf decoration based on the art and architecture of classical Egypt. They were cast in Leicester at the foundry of Samuel Wright. The lamp columns, decorated with ivy and olive leaf patterns, came originally from Paris, reputedly in the late 19th century. The same pattern is widely used in the French capital. Later columns were cast in Leicester but the ones used in an

improvement scheme in the 1990s were again imported from France. New Walk owes much of its present appearance to that series of improvement schemes from 1994 to 2005, funded by property owners, Leicester City Council, English Heritage and the Heritage Lottery Fund. Lost boundary walls and railings were replaced, including the big piers in front of the museum, and a new bound-gravel surface laid. The works also included a programme for treatment and replanting of trees continuing the life of New Walk as an urban avenue.

It is that green urban avenue that ties all the elements of New Walk together. By providing a car-free and pleasant route into the city centre, the walk is a glimpse of a better way of living in towns, even more important today than it was in the town of the early 19th century. Susanna Watts's sharp eye noted the sinuous curve of the walk and its steady uphill incline as it climbed towards the windmill by the toll gate. Today she might be surprised that New Walk is near the centre of a large city. But she may also note the diverse range of people who make New Walk a truly democratic space and reflect that her efforts to forge a better world in her own time had not been wasted.

New Walk, lamp column with ivy and olive leaf pattern

View over College Street, Highfields

SECTION **THREE**

VICTORIAN AND EDWARDIAN BOROUGH

The 19th century was pivotal in Leicester's history. Population grew by more than ten times and with it came the development of housing, industry, commerce, schools and churches, civic government and utilities. Leicester was still a mainly red brick and slate town but with a variety of building styles and materials.

Crescent Cottages

Chapter eight

Housing for the growing borough

Leicester grew from an estimated population of about 4,000 in 1500 to about 20,000 people by 1800: the size of a modest market town by modern standards.[65,66] But in 1901 the population of Leicester was 211,000, approaching the scale of the city of today.[67] The borough boundaries were extended to include what is now the inner city and inner suburbs in 1835. In 1892 the borough was again extended to include the parishes of Knighton, Aylestone and Belgrave.

Leicester was relatively forward looking in providing housing. Parliament had granted an act for enclosing the East Field in 1764, allowing former grazing land to be used for building by withdrawing the rights of established landowners. The corporation's long campaign to enclose the South Fields (see chapter 7) was successful in 1811 when enclosure was granted for that land also.

Enclosure ensured a supply of land for urban growth but much of the housing built on the land was in cramped one-up, one-down cottages built in confined streets, courtyards and infilled gardens. These covered much of the area of today's city centre and its fringes. Just one example of this type of housing remains from the slum clearance programmes of the mid-20th century. Cramant Cottages, built in about 1820, were tucked into a yard at the back of a property on King Street. Today the six cottages, together with a workshop, form a children's nursery and the little rooms adapt pleasantly to the needs of babies and toddlers. But in 1841, 22 people were crowded into the six tiny dwellings.[68]

Cramant Cottages, 1820s, converted in 1990s to a pub and later to a children's nursery

The corporation wasted no time in developing the South Fields. King Street was laid out between 1811 and 1813, and Wellington Street and Princess Road followed over the next five years. Development produced profits for the corporation and for its individual members. From the earliest streets nearest to the town, development continued south of Regent Road into the 1870s, forming a grid of rectangular plots developed in parcels by individual builders. The area was unified by the common use of mainly red brick, with occasional blocks in white brick or faced in stucco, and slate for roofing. Development was dominated by a neo-classical style, more varied than that of the Georgian town but retaining a consistent set of proportions, giving further unity to houses of varying ages.

The Crescent in King Street is one of the earliest of the grander buildings in the South Fields. William Firmadge, its architect, was himself a member of the corporation.[69] He used an orange-red brick, possibly from his own brickyard on Humberstone Road. The elegant, gentle curve of the frontage behind a row of mature trees and the fine ironwork porch and balcony make a formal composition relatively rare in Leicester.

LEFT AND TOP: *Crescent cottages*

The Crescent

ABOVE: *Upper King Street* **MIDDLE:** *Upper King Street*
FAR RIGHT: *Holy Trinity Church, corner of King Street and Regent Road*

The anthemion motif is much in evidence in the ironwork of The Crescent and on the houses on the opposite side of King Street and at numbers 1–5, 7 and 9–29 Upper King Street. Stucco came into fashion in Leicester as an outer covering in the early 19th century providing a smooth surface over possibly cheap brick and forming raised surrounds to doors and windows. The anthemion appears as an applied decoration on the giant pilasters.[70] William Flint designed the corner group, dated 1836, as a formal composition turning the angle into Regent Road, with a hinge-like end block neatly enclosed by spearhead railings.

The first Holy Trinity Church was a classical building designed by Sidney Smirke that would have complemented this well-mannered scene and the low roofline of Smirke's building can still be seen from Turner Street. In 1871 the church was radically remodelled to provide a complete contrast and a prominent end-stop to the southward view along King Street, one of the best street views in the area. The architect this time was Samuel Sanders Teulon, known for his radical and sometimes wilful interpretations of Gothic. At Holy Trinity he used a purple-brown brick with whitish and golden limestone and included tall French-inspired roofs.

NCELOT HOUSE

As the South Fields developed land was set aside for Welford Road Recreation Ground, Leicester's first public park, renamed in 1986 in honour of Nelson Mandela. The park sits under the imposing red brick walls of Leicester Prison.

The County Gaol was built in 1828 to the design of William Parsons, a contemporary and pupil of William Flint. The entrance range facing Welford Road is a Gothic sham-castle, built in light brown sandstone from Crich in Derbyshire.[71] The massive boundary walls with round buttresses and corner towers loom over residential streets but neither the building of the gaol nor the construction of the railway through the South Fields in 1835 stalled the development of the area. The South Fields continued to grow as a residential quarter with some distinctive houses like the simply-detailed 1830s classical pair at 10–12 Newtown Street and the secluded terrace at numbers 77–95 Regent Road, built in 1841.

To the east, South Highfields developed in a different way. A map of 1828 shows Prebend Street and a few houses fronting London Road before the railway cut through to the north of the area.[72] This part of South Highfields was developed by the Church and Commissioners who also laid out Conduit Street and Glebe Street. To the south the map shows the High Fields dotted with windmills; Mill Hill Lane winds towards Whetstone's Mill. The area attracted some large houses built in their own grounds but these were progressively replaced. Developers, including T M Evans, bought land and sold it on in plots in the north of the area in the 1860s, spreading southwards in the 1870s and 1880s, providing houses for the rising middle classes of the town. Some of the larger plots were later redeveloped pockets of small terraced housing forming the avenues that are a key part of the character of South Highfields.

FAR LEFT: *The County Gaol*
TOP LEFT: *Prison boundary Walk*
LEFT: *10-12 Newtown Street*
ABOVE: *77-95 Regent Road*

ABOVE: *College Street* **MIDDLE:** *Brookhouse Street* **TOP FAR RIGHT:** *Glebe Street* **BOTTOM FAR RIGHT:** *Victoria Avenue*

One of the earliest surviving houses in South Highfields, a dwelling of about 1828 at the junction of Prebend Street and Glebe Street, is Classical in style with finely-proportioned door and window openings, rather like some of the houses in the South Fields. It is built in red brick with a lighter brick forming a chequer pattern and is roofed in Swithland slate (see chapter 2).

Local materials were still important: Brookhouse Street and Victoria Avenue have expanses of pink Mountsorrel granite paving and kerbs for example. But the development of the railways opened up a much wider market for building materials. Welsh slate, lighter and cheaper than Swithland, became the predominant roofing material in Leicester and many other growing cities. The range of materials in South Highfields included orange-red Leicester brick, various stones for detailed

work like window and door surrounds, decorated moulded brick and coloured glazed tile. Architectural styles were diverse and included Gothic, Italian Renaissance and revived English styles.

Landmarks are important to the character of South Highfields, looming over rooftops, turning corners or closing vistas along streets. The tower of St Peters Church, built in 1872–74 to the design of George Edward Street, marks the north-eastern end of Highfield Street. The rather different landmark of the Marquis of Wellington pub of 1907, with its ornate coloured leadwork frontage, fills the view to the south-west.

GOTHAM STREET

GOTHA·HOUSE.

FAR LEFT: *Gotham Street and Highfield Street, brick and stucco*
MIDDLE: *Upper Tichborne Street* **ABOVE:** *Melbourne Hall Church*

COLLEGE STREET

The synagogue, designed by Arthur Wakerley (see chapter 15) and built in 1898, in Leicester red brick in a loose Romanesque style creating a distinctive identity expressed particularly by the copper onion-shaped dome: an echo of Russia or Eastern Europe. In Melbourne Road the big octagonal roof of Melbourne Hall Free Church, built in 1880, is a landmark on the horizon for much of the eastern part of the city.

Shops and flats at the junction of London Road and Highfield Street typify Arthur Wakerley's inventive architectural style. Built in 1888, they are in red brick with some decorative plasterwork and stone, a sequence of triangular and segmental gables on the skyline and a large inverted peardrop-shaped window looking northward.

The view towards the northern end of Prebend Street is closed by the former Collegiate School (now The Rowans) of 1836 designed by the Sheffield architect John Grey Weightman. Built in white brick and stone, its Gothic style and statues of notable Leicestershire Protestant figures seem to offer an Anglican response to the classical plainness of the Nonconformist Proprietary School in New Walk, which was built in the same year (see chapter 7).

FAR RIGHT: *The Rowans, former Collegiate School*
MIDDLE: *Leicester Hebrew Congregation Synagogue*
TOP RIGHT: *Leicester Hebrew Congregation Synagogue*
ABOVE: *Teardrop window by Arthur Wakerley, London Road*

View of Highfields

TOP LEFT: *St Saviours Road*
MIDDLE LEFT: *St Saviours Road*
LEFT: *St Saviours Road, window*

South Highfields has for many decades had an active and ethnically diverse community, reflected in the presence of the synagogue as early as the end of the 19th century. Turbulent passions at the time of the First World War are reflected in the restyling at that time of a number of streets which previously had German names.[73]

In the 1980s, the local community campaigned for the creation of

Fairfield Road

Prebend Gardens. It was part of a series of measures that followed the lifting of a threat to the area from major road proposals. Today places of worship, shops, restaurants and community centres serve Bangladeshi, Muslim, Somali, Sikh, Irish and other communities.

The Public Health Act of 1858 led to local bye-laws laying down minimum sizes for houses, including room sizes and dimensions of windows, with standards for street widths and yard areas.[74] Many hectares of land were built up with terraced housing governed by these standards, determining the built form of much of the inner part of the city. Thousands of these houses remain, proving resilient and adaptable to the needs of modern communities.

Leicester is not generally a hilly city, but from Melbourne Road the streets climb steeply towards Mere Road and the orange-red brick houses are stepped up the slope making a dramatic street scene. Wood Hill and Frederick Street were laid out in 1877 and many of the houses carry date-stones of the 1880s and 1890s, often with a little moulded brick decoration at the eaves and stone window and door heads.[75]

The regular rhythm of the terraced streets is moderated by larger buildings. St Saviours, built in 1875-77, is one of Sir George Gilbert Scott's four Leicester churches. Here he interpreted an early Gothic style from about 1200 in brick and, inside, white limestone with sturdy columns in red Shap granite from Cumbria.

Wesley Hall Methodist Church of 1896, the Imperial Hotel (originally a temperance establishment) and Spinney Hill Park opened in 1886, add to a picture of an integrated community life in the steep terraced streets.

The local school was another community landmark and a visual focus of the area. Charnwood Street School was built in 1876-77 for the Leicester School Board and, like many of the borough's board schools, was designed by Edward Burgess.

The school is a tall and imposing red brick building with red clay-tile roofs and a tower designed to draw air upward through the building. In 2009 a striking extension, designed by Maber Architects and clad in green laminate panels, was built on the west side of the site, facing the railway.

TOP RIGHT:
Westley Hall Methodist Church

RIGHT:
Wesley Hall Methodist Church

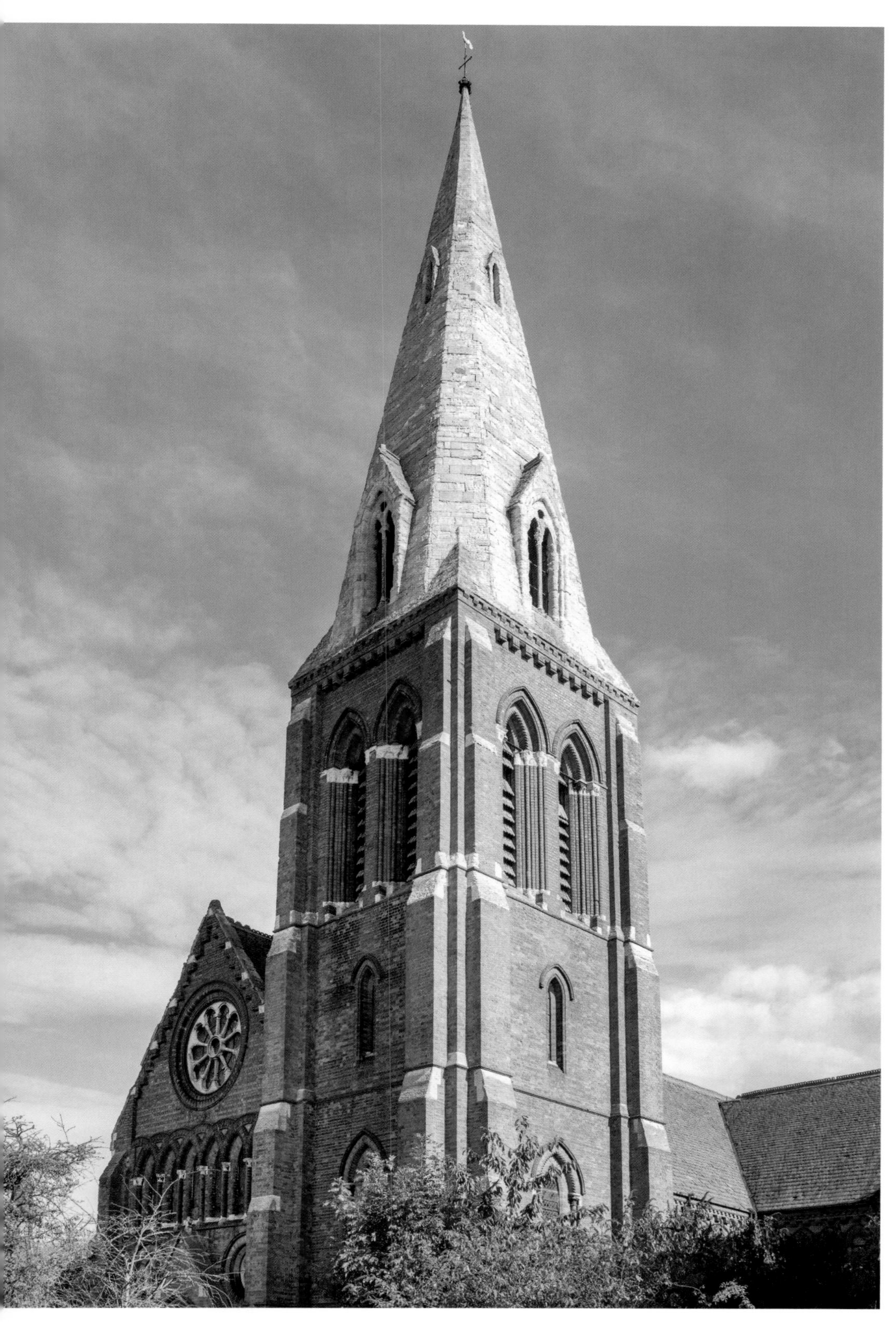

St Saviours Church

Former Apsara cinema is now the Masjid Usman mosque

Charnwood Street School

The school reflects the enduring importance of education for the succession of communities in the area. Melbourne Road is a thriving shopping street shaped by the energies of today's diverse community. The former Apsara cinema is now the Masjid Usman mosque and what was once the Melbourne Road Chapel is a Hindu centre: the Shree Samaj Sahayak Mandal.

All three areas described in this chapter owe the survival of their character to the renewal strategy carried out from the 1970s into the 1990s. This was a time of significant change in national thinking about the future of housing and a move away from demolition to the repair of older houses.

The renewal strategy was a partnership between Leicester City Council, housing associations and local residents that affected 35,000 properties, a third of Leicester's housing stock. In areas such as the South Fields and South Highfields, renewal was combined with conservation, helping to protect the architectural character of the area as well as extend the life of properties. Parallel programmes of environmental works and traffic management made streets more liveable. The renewal strategy was a programme of historic importance that changed the future of Leicester's housing stock and the communities who live in it.

Chapter nine

Work and enterprise

Britain was the first industrial country and industry drove the rapid growth of Leicester in the 19th century. Within recent memory, manufacturing was a major employer and streets resonated to the sound of machines. Factories were mixed with housing, churches, cinemas and pubs in the urban landscape. Although manufacturing still continues in Leicester it is on a much reduced scale.

Leicester's prosperity developed on the basis of a diverse range of industries but knitting and shoe manufacturing were pre-eminent. These industries gathered a supply chain of ancillary businesses so that the city was in itself like a great industrial process.[76] What survives of this time still shapes the character of Leicester. Many industrial buildings have found new uses and demonstrate the flexibility of some older industrial structures, extending the life of the energy and materials that went into building them and maintaining the street scenes that they created.

The riverside either side of West Bridge was a busy industrial area mainly making materials for the knitting industry. Donisthorpe's Friars Mill (taking its name from the priory of the Dominican Blackfriars in the north-west corner of the medieval town) was built around the turn of the 18th and 19th centuries for making worsted thread. The main mill building is an elegant classically-proportioned factory in orange-red brick. The ibex weather vane displayed the company's trademark.

City Mayor, Sir Peter Soulsby, took decisive action after a devastating fire in 2012 destroyed the roof. Levitate architects designed a scheme for the repair and reuse of the former factory as workspaces, as well as providing complementary new buildings and measures to conserve energy.

Friars Mill, restored 2012–16 after fire, with details of river frontage, roof structure, interior of cupola and new ibex weather vane

On the south side of West Bridge, the former Pex mill was also built for making worsted thread in about 1850. William Flint designed the building for John Whitmore and Sons. Taller and more imposing than Donisthorpe's but still classically inspired and built in orange-red brick, Flint's building has big overhanging eaves and an Italian-inspired campanile or bell tower. In the regeneration of the Pex site in the late 1990s, the main building was converted to offices with a modern glazed extension and lift tower. The scheme includes a public space which was linked to Castle Gardens by a new footbridge.

Moving further south, the area now dominated by the campus of De Montfort University would once have been an industrial community. Some of the factory buildings, like the Clephan Building of 1888 on Oxford Street, have been reused by the university. Others have found uses that complement the university's life.

The former Harrison and Hayes building on Gateway Street is now a pub and student housing. Built in 1913, it is one of the most original and decorative of Leicester's industrial buildings. The architect, S H Langley, chose a mixture of cream brick and green glazed brick with details sculpted in sandstone. The workshop range has a bold sense of function with arched gables and inverted arches.

ABOVE: *Pex mill, about 1850* **BELOW LEFT:** *Former Harrison and Hayes factory, stonework detail* **BELOW RIGHT:** *Former Harrison and Hayes factory, stonework detail*

Former Harrison and Hayes factory

ABOVE AND TOP RIGHT: *11-13 Wellington Stree*

The Luke Turner elastic webbing factory nearby in Henshaw Street was built in 1893. Stott and Sons architects of Oldham designed many industrial buildings in Lancashire over a period of about 100 years. The weight of the building is carried by an iron frame on the inside rather than on thick brick or stone walls. Metal or concrete frames became a normal way of constructing large buildings in the 20th century. The frame is clad on the outside with strips of wood or iron and the building has a light appearance with large expanses of glass. A now rare brick factory chimney survives in the yard behind the factory.

Industry extended well into the limits of the modern city centre, including the area between Granby Street and New Walk. Pictures of industrial buildings often adorned the advertisements and letterheads of their firms and the customers of companies at 11–13 Wellington Street must have been especially impressed. Built in around 1865, the frontage is broadly Venetian Gothic in style but includes a range of building materials and motifs. The Gothic arches on the ground floor have capitals with finely-carved plant forms and the basement openings are protected by ornate cast iron grilles. Above is a mixture of window openings, with materials including brick of several colours, stone and terracotta.

A group of red-brick former factory buildings around Stamford Street and York Street form a dramatic industrial street scene. The Briggs building of 1887–88, designed by Arthur Wakerley, has a monumental quality with red-brick pilasters rising through four storeys.

Briggs building, York Street

Cultural Quarter

The area around St Georges Church (now a Serbian Orthodox church) has the most diverse and distinctive collection of industrial and other buildings in the city centre. St Georges, built between 1823 and 1827, was the first Anglican church to be established in Leicester since the Reformation. William Parsons, better recognised as a classical architect, designed the church in the Decorated Gothic style. The main material is a yellowish sandstone but window tracery was made in cast iron, which is still sharply detailed, bringing an element of industrial production to a traditionally built church.

Street scenes in the St Georges area have a very distinctive quality formed by high buildings in relatively narrow streets. Corners of buildings are sometimes curved or angled to give extra emphasis or to incorporate a main entrance. Doorways and gateways are formed in contrasting materials, especially in stone.

There is a particularly imposing sequence of large buildings on the north side of Southampton Street. Two strong corners lead into Wimbledon Street where the looming height of St Georges Mills slants to close the view towards Humberstone Road in one of the city's best industrial street views. In Rutland Street the arc of Curve theatre leans dramatically into the vertical space of the street, making a foil to views of Alexandra House and the former Odeon cinema (now the Athena).

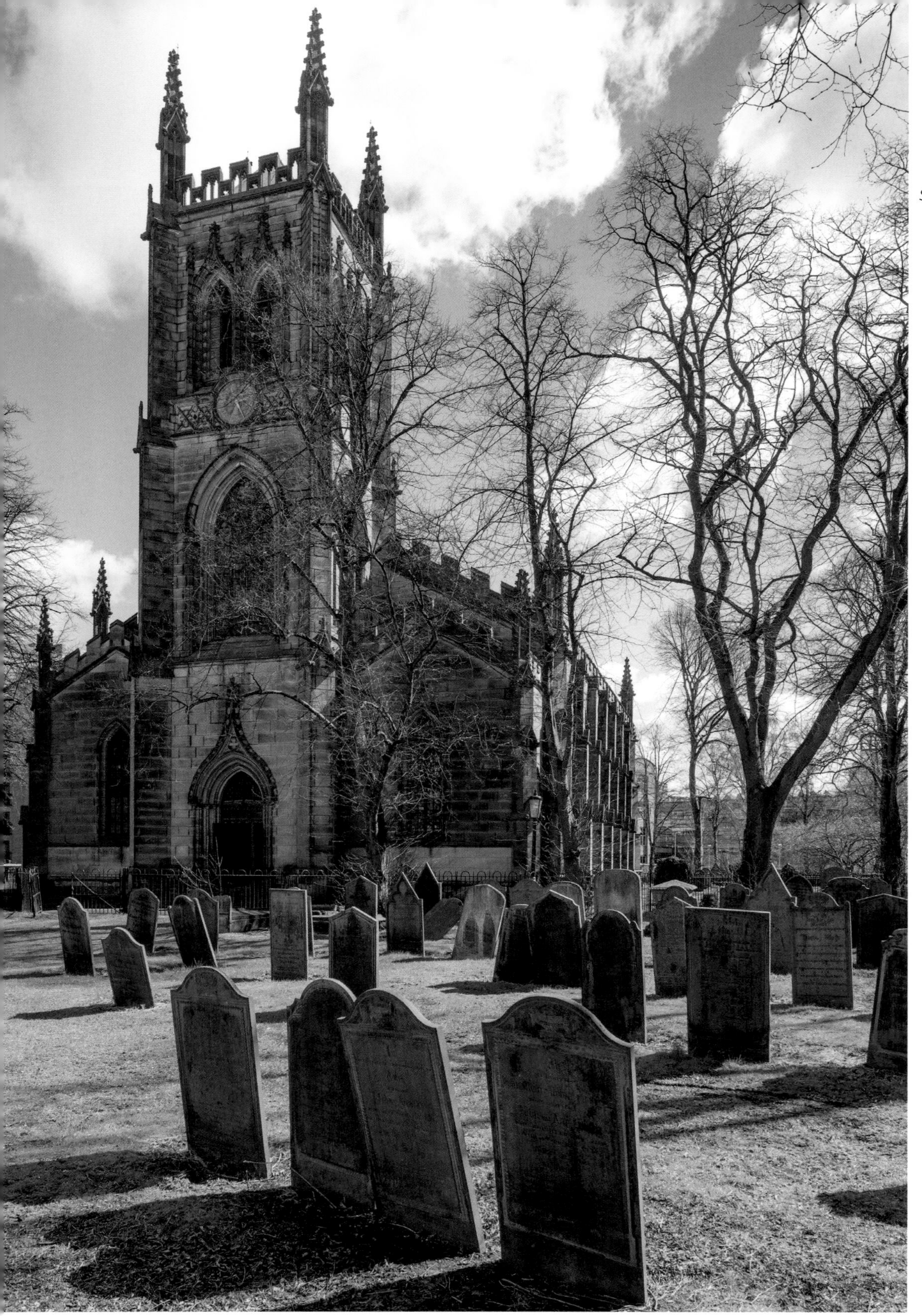

St Georges Church

Mortledge Street and Southampton Street

Premier House, at the corner of Colton Street and Rutland Street, is a bold four-storey warehouse originally built for Walter Dicks and Son, boot and shoe makers, in 1875. It is mainly built in a buff-yellow brick in an Italian-influenced style with a big overhang at the eaves and a curved corner bay. The speedy dispatch of Dicks's products is promised by figures, carved by Samuel Barfield, of Minerva clutching a railway engine and Mercury holding a ship.

The Athena event venue was converted from the original Odeon cinema in 2004–05, restoring the space of the auditorium which had been subdivided. The cinema's architect Harry Weedon devised a futuristic style for the Odeon chain of cinemas established by the Birmingham businessman Oscar Deutsch. The job architect for the Leicester Odeon, built in 1936–38 for 3,000 customers, was Robert Bullivant. His design complements its industrial neighbours in a completely original way. Two big projecting fins in brown brick breaking into facades of cream-glazed terracotta lead the eye around the corner of Queen Street and Rutland Street.

Numbers 82–96 Rutland Street are seen from the street as a simple three-storey red-brick frontage but the story of the building is complex. Until the middle of the 19th century, knitting was mainly a domestic industry: a framework knitter would have had a bulky knitting frame in their own house, perhaps in a room like those at Cramant Cottages (see chapter 8). Built in the 1850s, the building in Rutland Street could represent the earliest known surviving example of the move to factory production in the hosiery industry.[77]

Athena, former Odeon cinema

The factory had windows which, by the 1850s, had just two big panes of glass for each sash. Techniques of glass production had advanced by the mid-19th century compared with the technology that produced the small-paned Georgian windows (see chapter 6). The bigger panes were heavy and required the additions of horns (vertical extensions to the side rails) to make a stronger, closed joint.

Numbers 82–96 Rutland Street reopened in 2013 as Makers Yard, a cluster of craft workspaces. The conversion scheme by Maber Architects allowed for the retention of machinery and even internal finishes as well as providing a new lift and stair tower.

Many of the former industrial buildings in the St Georges area are now in residential or mixed use and this is the case at 78–80 Rutland Street. The building was originally a warehouse for Pfister and Vogel, an American leather company based in Milwaukee and it was built in 1923. The collection of architectural motifs on the frontage do not really add up to a style. The pointed arch over the left-hand doorway suggests a Gothic inspiration but the building has a concrete frame that allows large window openings, giving it a distinctly 20th century appearance. It may have been influenced by one of the company's premises in the United States but its architects Fosbrooke and Bedingfield (Thomas Henry Fosbrooke and Waller King Bedingfield) used similar Gothic details on industrial buildings of the time elsewhere in

Leicester. White limestone and green-glazed brick are used on the front of the building. But the rear, visible from Yeoman Street, is startlingly modern with four and a half floors of glazing.

FAR LEFT: *82–96 Rutland Street, Makers Yard*
MIDDLE TOP: *Makers Yard, interior*
MIDDLE BOTTOM: *Makers Yard, internal courtyard with new work, 2012–13*
RIGHT: *78–80 Rutland Street*

47
ALEXANDRA HOUSE

LEFT: *Alexandra House* **ABOVE:** *Alexandra House, detail of atlas bracket*

A diversion from Rutland Street illustrates a different industrial story. The Boot and Shoe Operatives Trade Union built their national headquarters in St James's Street in 1902. The frontage is in a free Classical style with four big Corinthian pilasters in buff Hollington limestone from Staffordshire, rising through the first and second floors. The Art Nouveau ironwork was made by Gimson and Company.[78]

The star of a strong cast of buildings around Curve is Alexandra House, designed by Edward Burgess as a bootlace warehouse for Faire Brothers. It was built in 1897 in an extravagant Baroque style including shell-like arches over window openings and, most eye-catching, a line of atlantes[135] supporting the main cornice.[79, 80, 81] The buff moulded terracotta was made by the Burmantofts company of Leeds and the contrasting plinth is larvikite, a dark-grey, granite-like stone from Norway. The fibreglass corner dome on Alexandra House is a replacement for the original one which was destroyed in a fire caused by bombing in 1941.

After the First World War, building costs increased and building technology advanced. As chapter 18 will show, industrial buildings became more utilitarian, leaving Alexandra House as a highpoint of confidence and style in Leicester's industrial architecture.

ABOVE: *Originally the Leicestershire Bank , now International Society of Krishna Consciousness (ISKCON)*
ABOVE RIGHT: *Detail of moulded brick and stonework, ISKCON*

Chapter ten

Commerce

Victorian Leicester's industrial wealth sustained a wider economy of banks, shops, cafés and hotels. Granby Street and High Street each contain a sequence of monuments to the commercial confidence and prosperity of the 19th century borough.

Two banks epitomise much of this self-assurance as well as the underlying tensions within the Victorian borough. William Millican designed the National Provincial Bank (now NatWest) for the corner of Granby Street and Horsefair Street. Opened in 1869, it is built in Portland limestone and yellowish-buff brick. The style is derived from that of a palazzo of a Florentine merchant or from one of the London gentlemen's clubs being built at the time. The solid quality of the building is typified by the long rusticated quoins flanking the corner entrance.[82]

Joseph Goddard was a younger man than Millican and of rival religious and political persuasions. The year 1869 saw him also designing a bank nearby on the corner of Granby Street and Bishop Street for the Leicestershire Banking Company. Goddard's drawings show that he began working in a similar Italianate style to Millican, but he then changed to a part-Italianate, part-Gothic scheme and then again to a complete free Gothic style with a French pavilion roof over the main corner entrance.[83, 84] Inside the flowing patterns of the coloured glasswork seem to anticipate the Art Nouveau style by several decades. The range of materials echoes the originality of the design with red brick, white limestone (carved by Goddard's favoured sculptor Samuel Barfield), moulded terracotta and iron railings. Goddard created one of Leicester's most distinctive buildings and one that has now been adapted to a completely different use as a centre for the International Society of Krishna Consciousness (ISKCON).

MIDDLE TOP: *ISKCON, detail of banking hall windows* **MIDDLE LEFT:** *ISKCON, detail of banking hall windows* **ABOVE:** *ISKCON, detail of banking hall windows*

Former Victoria Coffee House, 38-40 Granby Street

Former General News Room, Granby Street

Two cafés tell another story of the Victorian borough. The Victoria Coffee House at 38–40 Granby Street was designed by Edward Burgess and built in 1888. Burgess's design is in a free baroque style built in a yellowish-buff sandstone. The architect was involved in the coffee house movement, an expression of Victorian social reform, and the ornate exteriors of the coffee houses were intended to tempt working men into places of refreshment that offered an alternative to the pubs.

Arthur Wakerley's (see chapter 15) design for Turkey Café of 1900 is flamboyant in a different way. The Turkey Café is one of Leicester's best examples of coloured glazed terracotta or *faience* and one of its buildings most influenced by Art Nouveau, a style that was never really popular in England as it was in other parts of Europe. The main panels were made by the Royal Doulton company in London in a material marketed as Carraraware. They were designed for Doulton by William Neatby. Inside the café there is a tiled mural panel from the 1960s with another variation on the turkey theme and the ground-floor arch is supported by *faience* turkeys sculpted and made at Hathernware Ceramics as part of a restoration scheme in the 1980s.

Henry Langton Goddard designed a number of buildings in Leicester and elsewhere in a revived version of the baroque style. The building on the corner of Granby Street and Belvoir Street was built as the General News Room in 1898 and is faced in Burmantofts terracotta. This is an elaborate example of baroque: the concave corner bay, statues and windows recessed between columns give the building a sense of restless movement compared with the stable classical calm of a structure like the New Walk Museum portico.

LEFT: *Turkey Café, Granby Street*
TOP: *Restored turkey corbel made by Hathernware Ceramics*
ABOVE RIGHT: *Detail of Carraraware column*
ABOVE LEFT: *Detail of Turkey Café*

GRAND
HOTEL
Alex Clark Lettings
Alex Clark Lettings
CITY SURPLUS
Text & Talk

Mercure Leicester
The Grand Hotel

In the later 17th century, English architecture developed its own distinctive variation on the Baroque style. Baroque was then revived at the end of the 19th century. The Grand Hotel, the first phase of which was built in 1896, is in a mix of styles including Flemish as well as Baroque, developed over several phases of construction. The corner tower, designed by architect Cecil Ogden with Simpson and Harvey, echoes churches built by Sir Christopher Wren after the 1666 Great Fire of London. Flemish gables, turrets and the Portland stone corner tower give the building a varied and lively skyline.

Further south along Granby Street there is a mix of styles and sculptural details including a Flemish stepped gable on the corner of Chatham Street and decorative ironwork at number 80. The YMCA building of 1901 has a strange and slightly sinister collection of crouching winged figures sculpted in stone in the upper corners of the first-floor windows.

ABOVE TOP : *Grand Hotel, detail of fireplace* **ABOVE MIDDLE:** *Grand Hotel, interior staircase*
ABOVE: *Grand Hotel, interior door head*

YMCA building, East Street

The High Street (medieval Swines Market) was a historic street which was widened in 1902 to make way for tram tracks. King James I and King Charles I stayed at the Lord's Place, a grand house on the north side built for Henry Earl of Huntingdon in 1569. Mary, Queen of Scots was imprisoned there in 1586. The Huntingdon Tower, the last remnant of the house, was demolished in 1902 and the site is now commemorated only by a memorial plaque on the building that replaced it.

High Street retained much of the consistency of form established by the early 20th century rebuilding. It is straight and focuses on the Clock Tower at the site of the Roman and medieval East Gate. Rebuilding produced a regular street frontage but great variety in building styles and materials, and a striking skyline with a sequence of extravagantly shaped gables on both sides. Some on the north side were built in the early 1990s as a lively post-modern addition to the street.[85] Since 2008, High Street has been a mainly pedestrian street with the atmosphere of a relaxed city boulevard. The reconstruction after 1902 produced a series of big architectural personalities, none more so than Coronation Buildings at numbers 76-86. Built for the Singer Sewing Machine Company between 1902 and 1904, the building shows Arthur Wakerley's architecture at its most flamboyant and reflects the high point of imperial confidence. Wakerley made liberal use of Doulton Carraraware making Union Jack roundels, each topped by an animal representing part of the British Empire, abstract chequer patterns and pictorial panels of ships sailing out to distant lands.

YMCA building, detailed sculptures and window heads

Coronation Buildings, 76–86 High Street

On the corner of Carts Lane, the architect AE Sawday also made colourful use of glazed ceramics, this time in a more modest building. Here the ceramic panels advertise Sea Breeze headache cure which was made on the site. Most shops have lost their original shopfronts and the harmony between ground and upper floors has gone. But 60 High Street has an original shopfront with delicate cast iron uprights, curved glass panels and a suggestion of Art Nouveau in the design of the door.

The street view along Carts Lane, framed by this building, takes the eye right through the medieval core of the town to the little dome of the Poor Law Offices (see chapter 11), beyond the line of the southern stretch of the town walls.

Lloyds Bank, on the north side at 9 High Street, is calmly classical with a flat skyline and an Ionic colonnade on the ground floor in grey Cornish granite with white limestone above.[86] The Birmingham architect J A Chatwin was favoured by Lloyds and, like the example in High Street built in 1903-06, many of his banks are in a rigorous Italian-inspired style. The bank is a successor to one founded in 1825 by the prominent Leicester banker and politician Thomas Paget.

TOP: *Coronation Building, 76–86 High Street, glazed tile*

RIGHT: *Leadwork, terracotta and glazed tile, former premises of TE Butler and Son, Chemists, 58 High Street*

Lloyds Bank, 9 High Street

Arcades, forerunners of the modern shopping mall, were a trend in British cities in the later 19th century.[87] Silver Arcade was built in 1899 to the design of Amos Hall. The buildings fronting Silver Street and Cank Street are in a baroque style in yellowish sandstone: the Silver Street frontage is particularly showy with obelisks set in arched, open-topped pediments. Arcades made use of the backs of plots and allowed free movement between streets through a privately-owned gallery. Customers were tempted to linger in Silver Arcade in a space adorned by ironwork, shopfronts, lanterns and friezes of plump cherubs. The small units have always catered for specialised interests, one of the essential aspects of a varied city centre. The arcade has yet to become busy again following a refurbishment in 2010 designed by Boden Associates of Nottingham.

Every Leicester citizen has a place in their heart for the Clock Tower. Once in the middle of a traffic island, the tower is now the centre of a pedestrian space and a real focal point of the city centre. It is not Leicester's most accomplished piece of architecture, but for older citizens the Clock Tower is the emotional heart of the city and it provides a meeting place for young people before they head off to shops or cafés.

The origin of the Clock Tower is more matter of fact. It was built in 1868 at the junction of several of the borough's sewers and provided access to them. Its architect was the prolific Joseph Goddard, working with the sculptor Samuel Barfield who made the statues of William Wyggeston, Sir Thomas White, Simon de Montfort and Gabriel Newton. The tower is built in whitish Lincolnshire limestone with small columns in red shap granite.

RIGHT: *Former Eastgates Coffee House, The Clock Tower, Sporting Success*
BELOW: *Silver Arcade*

BELOW: *Clock Tower statues from top:Gabriel Newton, Simon De Montfort, Sir Thomas White, William Wyggeston. The architect Joseph Goddard may have been the model for Newton, De Montfort and Wyggeston*

ABOVE: *Panels illustrate events in the history of the Thomas Cook company*
LEFT: *Thomas Cook building*

The Clock Tower is complemented by several good historic buildings. The Eastgates Coffee House, built in 1885, perhaps echoes a 16th-century market building in Shropshire or Cheshire. The arched ground floor is a modern interpretation of its original design installed by a new owner in 1996. The Eastgates Coffee House forms a bookend with another of Burgess's coffee houses built at the junction with Highcross Street at the western end of High Street in 1895.

The Thomas Cook building at the northern end of Gallowtree Gate, another product of the Goddard practice, was built in 1894. The baroque façade incorporates panels showing landmarks in the development of Cook's travel business. Opposite, Martin Williams's bronze sculpture, Sporting Success, celebrates a marvellous year for Leicester teams in 1996–1997.

On either side of Victoria Passage there is an opportunity to compare brick bonds: the pattern with which the bricks bind through the thickness of the wall. On the south side is a purplish red brick laid in English bond made by alternate rows of stretchers (the long edge of a brick) and headers (the short edge). This

RIGHT:
Eastgates Coffee House

bond was standard in the Tudor period then revived in the later 19th century. On the opposite building an orange-red brick is laid in Flemish bond, which began to replace English bond from the 17th century and became widely used because of its strength and economy. In Flemish bond, headers and stretchers alternate within each row producing the familiar cross pattern.

Chapter eleven

Civic pride

Bishop Street Methodist Church was built in 1815 near the southern edge of the growing town and overlooking the borough cattle market in a very different setting from the civic scene it forms part of today. The church was designed by Rev William Jenkins in a refined classical style and built in red brick with a little stonework.

The need for new civic offices had long been recognised as the administration of a fast growing borough outgrew the Guildhall. The new Town Hall was subject to a complex and controversial process of design competitions. National and local architects entered schemes in a variety of styles.[88]

The winner was surprising. Francis John Hames was born in Leicester. He designed a building in Silver Street and worked in London but little else is known of him. Hames was by then working with the much better known London architect William Eden Nesfield and the Town Hall, opened in 1876, appears to be closely influenced by Nesfield's work in the Queen Anne style. The plain, formal style evolved in the time of Queen Anne in the early 18th century and was revived in a freely adapted form in the mid to late 19th century. Other cities built much more bombastic town halls in Gothic or baroque styles but Leicester's choice was calm and civilised and built in warm Suffolk red brick and golden Ketton limestone from Rutland.

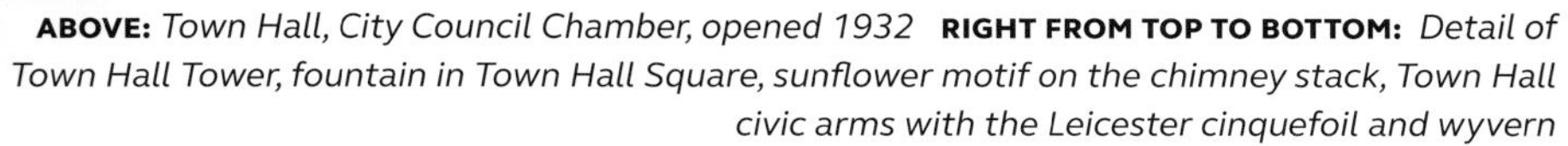

ABOVE: *Town Hall, City Council Chamber, opened 1932* **RIGHT FROM TOP TO BOTTOM:** *Detail of Town Hall Tower, fountain in Town Hall Square, sunflower motif on the chimney stack, Town Hall civic arms with the Leicester cinquefoil and wyvern*

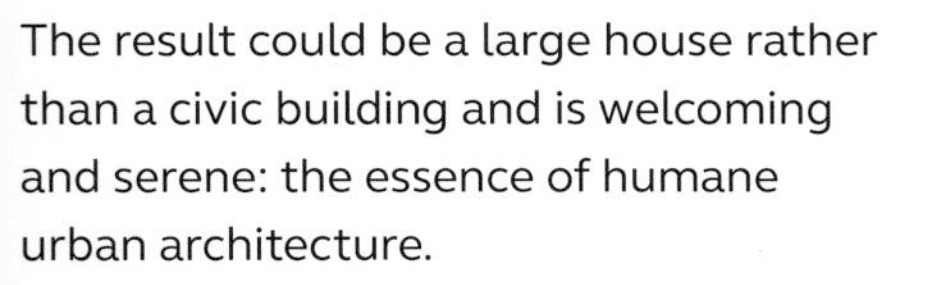

The result could be a large house rather than a civic building and is welcoming and serene: the essence of humane urban architecture.

The tower of the Town Hall is a landmark in distant views into and from within the city. The sunflower motif, a signature of the Queen Anne style in Leicester and elsewhere, is much in evidence in moulded brick. The foundation stone panels display a sculpted owl representing night and, less obviously, a duck heralding day. The civic arms with the Leicester cinquefoil are blazoned on the large curved gable, topped by the Leicester wyvern which takes the entrance bay up to the skyline.

The Town Hall, Town Hall Square and fountain

TOP: *Oval fanlight and segmental pediment, Horsefair Street elevation, Town Hall*

MIDDLE: *The owl representing night, Town Hall Square elevation, Town Hall*

BOTTOM: *Wyvern niche, Horsefair Street elevation, Town Hall*

The cattle market moved to Freemen's Common in 1876 and the mess and noise of the market gave way to a new civic space designed by Hames, giving us what is now Town Hall Square. The present layout of the square, with a mainly traffic-free space in front of the Town Hall, was designed by the city council and formally opened in 1989. It is a centre of the city's life, enjoyed by sunbathers and lunchtime strollers and often enlivened by wedding parties.

Sir Israel Hart, a former mayor of Leicester, gave the fountain at the centre of the square as a gift to the borough. Hames designed the fountain and it was cast in Paris. At least one other cast was made and an identical fountain stands in the city of Porto in Portugal. The winged Assyrian lions and Ionic columns were cast in iron and painted bronze and the fountain also uses two types of granite.

The Boer War Memorial in the north-eastern corner of the square was unveiled in 1909 after a long delay caused by fruitless negotiations with one of the leading sculptors of the day, Sir Alfred Gilbert.

Joseph Crosland McClure of Leicester Municipal School of Art eventually stepped in to make the Art Nouveau-inspired figure sculptures which were cast in bronze at the Singer foundry in Somerset and set on a grey granite plinth.[89]

ABOVE: *Interior of Bishop Street, Methodist Church*
TOP LEFT: *East side of Town Hall Square, Former Barclays Bank, former Pickford's Building, rear elevation of 7–9 Granby Street*
RIGHT: *Boer War Memorial, Town Hall Square*

In honour of
those that perish
in the war
please treat
the Memorial an
surrounding
area with respec

Former Poor Law offices, Pocklington's Walk

ABOVE: *Former Water Board Offices, Bowling Green Street*
RIGHT: *Former Constitutional Club, Pocklington's Walk*

Development around the square in a variety of styles and materials provided the Town Hall with an imposing urban setting.

On Bowling Green Street the extension to the back of the Town Hall was built in the 1920s in a style complementary to Hames's Queen Anne. It encloses the street, framing a splendid street view looking south to the curved outer wall of Hansom's Belvoir Street Chapel, built in 1845.

The Town Hall stands within a cluster of civic buildings in Bowling

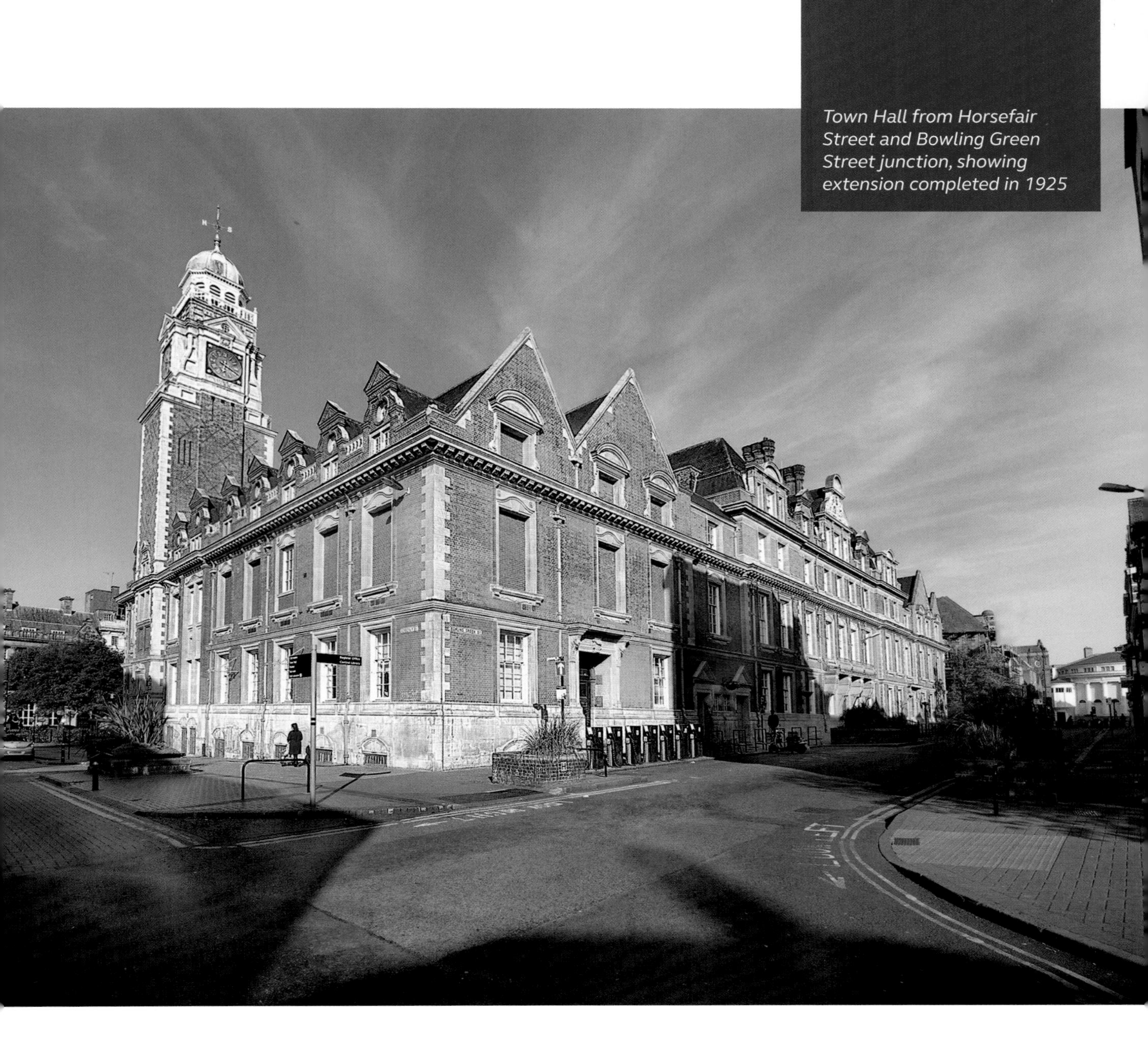

Town Hall from Horsefair Street and Bowling Green Street junction, showing extension completed in 1925

reen Street and Pocklington's Walk. he Water Board Offices at number Bowling Green Street are built in ed brick and a creamy limestone. he architects, Shenton and Baker hose a Gothic style unusual for civic uildings in Leicester. In Pocklington's Valk's the former Constitutional Club, later brought into civic use, is an elaborate mix of Flemish and French Renaissance style in orange-red brick and golden limestone. Next to it are the Poor Law Offices, for many years the city's Register Office, built in 1883 to the design of Redfern and Sawday (Francis Redfern b. 1877), built in a civic Italianate style in red brick and yellowish limestone.

Chapter twelve

Welford Road Cemetery

The burial of the dead led to serious problems in many 19th century cities as the overcrowding of churchyards became a threat to public health. Urban cemeteries were developed as a solution, many of them influenced by the Scottish landscape architect John Claudius Loudon who designed cemeteries himself and published books and articles on garden and cemetery design. The designers of Welford Road Cemetery, Hamilton and Medland, were among the many who absorbed Loudon's idea of cemeteries as picturesque landscapes for strolling and reflection, as well as for the practical purposes of burying the dead and providing solace for the bereaved.

Welford Road Cemetery was opened by the Leicester Cemetery Company on 19 June 1849: the same day as the launch of New Walk Museum. Separate areas were set aside for Anglicans and Nonconformists, with gatelodges and separate Gothic chapels for the denominations. Only the lodge on University Road remains, now extended, as The Gatehouse, opened in 1991 as the chaplaincy centre for the University of Leicester.

Much of the picturesque landscape survives, including some of the specimen trees that were part of the original planting scheme. On the gentle slope towards the railway, areas of flower-filled meadow provide habitat for a diverse range of insect species that in turn attract birds and mammals; the cemetery is managed accordingly as a Site of Importance for Nature Conservation.

Welford Road Cemetery is an important key to the city's history. Many of the leading citizens of the Victorian and Edwardian borough are buried there.

Welford Road Cemetery, landscape looking west from the chapels area

Some figure in this book or in the recorded history of the city; others are less well remembered.

The memorials were made in a wide variety of styles: Gothic, classical, Art Nouveau, Celtic and Moorish and in a diverse range of stones. Appropriately for sober, Nonconformist Leicester, many important figures are commemorated by simple, unassuming headstones. Exceptions include the Harris family tombs in the south-west corner of the cemetery, which are an elaborate group including a square column supporting a veiled urn and flanking classical temples with lotus-leaf capitals to the columns. The Wakerley family memorial beside the terrace west of the site of the chapels is a column with Art Nouveau angels delicately carved in a gritty red sandstone.

The cemetery contains the graves and memorials of casualties of the First World War who died in Leicester. After the Second World War the city became home to communities from Eastern Europe and some of the people who arrived in Leicester at that time are now commemorated in the cemetery, often with shiny granite headstones.

An active friends group has researched the cemetery records and located the graves of some of the most important figures. These are recorded on a series of steel tablets in the chapels area and maps show the locations of the graves that are highlighted. Attitudes to the cemetery have changed since the time of its Victorian founders but it remains a beautiful and fascinating place where visitors can still reflect on the place of the individual within the relentless advance of time and history.

ABOVE: *The Harris family monuments*

BELOW: *Decorative memorials in the cemetery*

Memorial sculpture

The grave of Thomas Cook (d.1892)

Chapter thirteen

Services for the borough

Georgian towns are idealised in literature but living in them was another matter. Sewage would have been discharged into cesspits and from there into the ground or it would be collected after dark by nightmen.[90] This situation lasted well into the 19th century but much better services were necessary for urban growth and these developed in response to a growing body of national and local laws, including the great reforms of the Public Health Act of 1875. Growing needs for services were met by a Victorian genius for invention and innovation, both by private companies and by modernising local authorities. Gas, electricity, water, transport and particularly sewers made the development of Victorian towns and cities possible.

Leicester began to build a network of sewers from the middle of the 19th century and in 1885 the corporation bought land at Beaumont Leys to construct a treatment works for the borough's sewage. The land was higher than the town and moving the sewage up the hill needed a system of pipes and pumps which were designed by the borough surveyor Joseph Gordon.[91] The motive power was provided by Abbey Pumping Station, built between 1887 and 1891, the design of which shows the borough's pride in the progress that the system represented. The architect Stockdale Harrison designed the building: a tall, sturdy structure in pinkish red brick and buff sandstone with a prominent roof light and a tall chimney. The four massive engines were built by Gimson and Company and are monumental in scale and decorative quality. The four flywheels are supported by a structure carried on paired cast iron Corinthian columns with acanthus-leaf bases.[92] When the engines are operated they fill the building with sound, steam and a palpable energy.

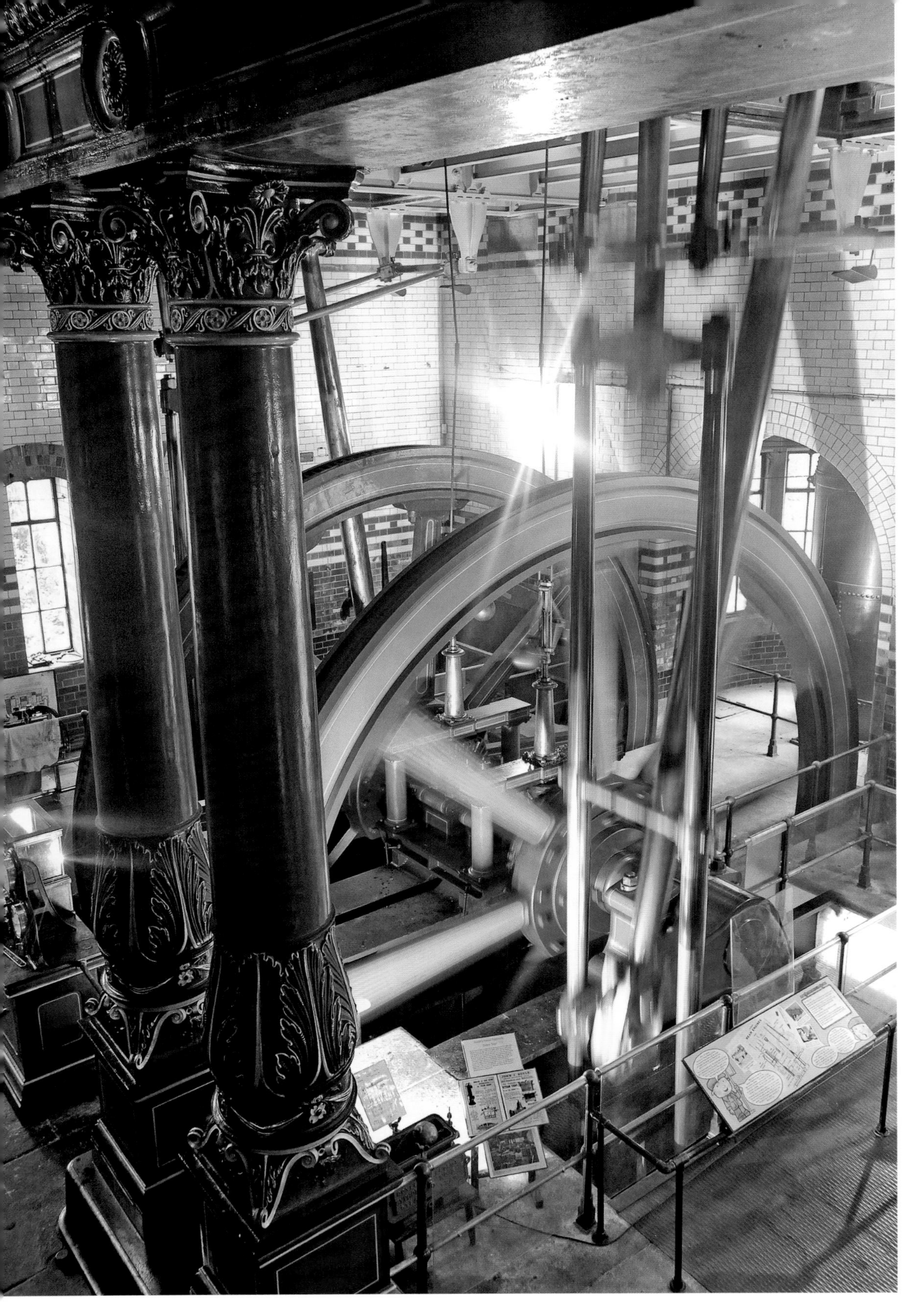

FAR LEFT: *Abbey Pumping Station, chimney*
MIDDLE: *Abbey Pumping Station*
RIGHT: *Abbey Pumping Station, pumping engines built by Gimson and Co*

Gas workers' cottages, Aylestone Road

Tower, Gas Museum

From as early as 1821, the borough had gas lighting produced from coal by the Leicester Gas-Light and Coke Company at its works in Belgrave Gate. Gas proved to be expensive and risky and the corporation eventually took over the company in 1878. The gasworks at Aylestone Road, sited with good access by road and canal, was begun in 1875 and expanded as the size of the enterprise grew.

The architects Shenton and Baker designed a set of buildings at Aylestone Road, including a terrace of workers' houses in an idealised style based on English cottage architecture. The building that now houses the Gas Museum with its tall red-brick clock tower, buff sandstone dressings and liberal use of moulded brick rosettes, also reflects pride in the development of local services.[93]

Railways had a huge impact on the shaping and reshaping of 19th century cities. Leicester's first railway ran to Swannington from a station on the land now known as Rally Park near Tudor Road. The line was built by Robert Stephenson in 1832. One of Stephenson's feats of engineering on the line was the mile-long Glenfield Tunnel. The structure largely survives including one entrance portal (outside the city) and a number of ventilation shafts.

Tower, Gas Museum

ABOVE: *Statue of Thomas Cook* **TOP CENTRE:** *Leicester Railway Station, detail* **TOP RIGHT:** *19 Midland Railway arms, containing emblems of Birmingham, Derby, Bristol, Leicester, Lincoln and Leeds, railway bridge, London Road* **TOP MIDDLE RIGHT:** *Midland Railway initials, railway bridge, London Road* **BOTTOM:** *Detail of faience Arrival arch*

The first rail connections to London (and progressively to other national destinations) departed from a station in Campbell Street which opened in 1840. A pair of sandstone gatepiers in Station Street is all that remains of the splendid classical station building designed by William Parsons. A bronze statue of Thomas Cook by James Butler was unveiled in 1993 close both to London Road station and to the earlier station from which Cook's first tour departed for Loughborough in 1841, commemorating Leicester's particular contribution to the history of travel. The red telephone box was a design classic common to places throughout the length of Britain. Leicester's two remaining post office telephone boxes stand outside the station on London Road. The K6 box (there were seven types in all) was designed by Giles Gilbert Scott in 1935 but used for many years afterwards. Scott was influenced in his design for the K6 by Sir John Soane's house in London.

From the 1880s, the Midland Railway rebuilt its main stations and the present station came into use from 1892. The company's architect, Charles Trubshaw, designed many of the new stations including those at Nottingham and Sheffield. The platform areas were completely rebuilt in the 1970s but Trubshaw's busy *porte-cochère*, with its clock tower, tall arches and Burmantofts terracotta panels announcing Arrival and Departure, serves to remind us of the Victorian excitement in travel and fast-developing technology, of the enjoyment of anticipating a journey and of the pleasure at returning home.[94]

Porte-cochère and clock tower, Leicester railway station, London Road, with K6 telephone boxes made to a design of 1935

FASTER TO
LONDON
GET ON BOARD

Inside the porte-cochère, Leicester Railway Station, London Road

Chapter fourteen

Suburban cross-section

The south-eastern suburbs: Clarendon Park, Stoneygate and South Knighton, running along either side of London Road, became a favoured location for Victorian business and professional people who built large, well-designed and solid houses, often standing in spacious gardens. Trees are a key part of the character of the area, enclosing views and providing a green contrast to brick and tile. Areas of terraced housing were also built in the south-eastern suburbs and, from the early phases of development in the area, plots have been subdivided. Later, large houses were turned into flats and some sites were developed for new flats or for student housing.

Joseph Goddard's architecture did much to shape the qualities of the

FAR LEFT: *103–105 Princess Road East* **LEFT:** *103 Princess Road East, detail of porch*
ABOVE: *107 Princess Road East, corbel detail on chimney* **RIGHT:** *105 and 107 Princess Road East, roofline*

south-eastern suburbs. But it is in a location now quite close to the city centre, at 12 University Road, where he built a house for himself in 1875–76.[95] Nearby, on the south side of Princess Road East between West Walk and University Road, there is a small group of typical Goddard houses. Their style is based on a revival of earlier English styles, especially Queen Anne. The houses are built in red brick with Welsh slate roofs and big brick chimney stacks. Some have timber porches and decoration in stone or moulded brick. Inside there are examples of beautiful coloured glass in doors or staircase windows.

LEFT AND ABOVE: *Landsdowne House, 113 Princess Road East*

LEFT AND ABOVE: *12 University Road and details*

Terracotta dragon finial

12 Knighton Park Road

Across Victoria Park, number 12 Knighton Park Road was built in 1882 for Wilmot Pilsbury, first headmaster of the Leicester College of Art and Technology, and includes an artist's studio.[96] Pilsbury's architect was another of the figures who shaped the character of the south-eastern suburbs, Isaac Barradale. The house in Knighton Park Road is an example of some of the characteristic features of his style: built in red brick with red clay-tile roofs, black-and-white timber framing and plasterwork, in this case with incised patterns. The house also has a terracotta roof finial in the form of a dragon: a quirky decoration that appears on several houses around the southeastern suburbs.

Ernest Gimson was one of Leicester's most important creative figures. He was a man of multiple talents and a leading member of the Arts and Crafts movement.[97] He trained as an architect with Barradale before moving to London as a pupil of John Dando Sedding. His legacy in Leicester is becoming better understood and New Walk Museum has a display of Gimson furniture and decorative art. Gimson's two houses in the city are private but Stoneywell Cottage at Ulverscroft is owned and managed by the National Trust and has been open to the public since 2015.

Doorway, Knighton Park Road

15 Knighton Park Road

Brookfield, London Road

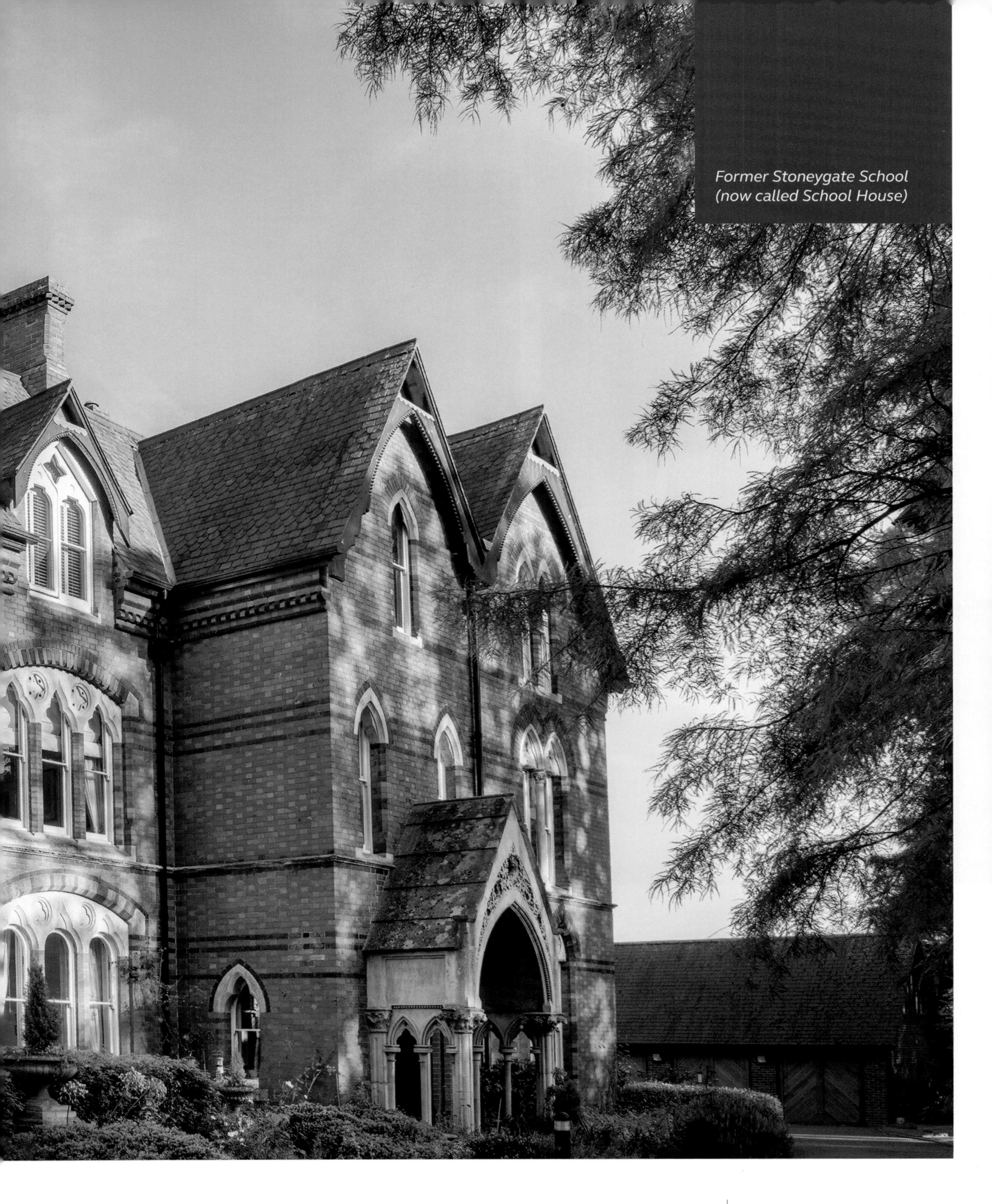
Former Stoneygate School (now called School House)

Houses by Isaac Barradale

The Firs, London Road

The White House in North Avenue was built for Gimson's brother Arthur in 1895–97. It is strikingly unadorned compared with Barradale's house nearby. The big prow facing North Avenue is a particularly notable and original feature. Built in plain limewashed brick with deep Swithland slate roofs, the White House has only modest external decoration in the form of curved gutter brackets, moulded rainwater heads and, facing the garden, decorative plasterwork by George Percy Bankart. Bankart was a friend of Gimson's and a fellow pupil at Barradale's office who went on to specialise in plaster and leadwork.[98]

On London Road there are three buildings that provide keys to the development of the south-eastern suburbs. On the east side, opposite the end of Knighton Park Road, Stoneygate School (now School House) is attributed to John Henry Chamberlain, an architect born in Leicester and trained by Henry Goddard. Chamberlain moved to Birmingham where he became a major figure closely associated with the civic reforms of the (unrelated) mayor Joseph Chamberlain. Stoneygate School was

The White House, North Avenue

Barradale houses, Clarendon Park Road

The White House, detail of gutter brackets and Swithland slate

built in 1859 in a domestic Gothic style in red brick with blue brick bands and decorative details in limestone, perhaps carved by Samuel Barfield who Chamberlain also worked with in Birmingham.

Immediately to the south Brookfield, built in 1876–78 to the design of Joseph Goddard, marks the reintroduction of black-and-white timber framing into Victorian Leicester for the first time. Further south on the west side The Firs at 223 London Road is a simply-detailed, Classical, stucco-fronted house of 1829. It was built in countryside but now marks an early phase in the development of the south-eastern suburbs.

Clarendon Park Congregational Church, London Road

Clarendon Park Congregational Church, leaded lantern and gables

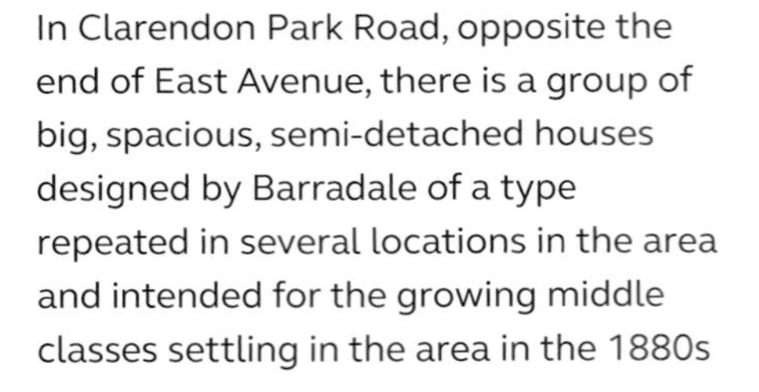

In Clarendon Park Road, opposite the end of East Avenue, there is a group of big, spacious, semi-detached houses designed by Barradale of a type repeated in several locations in the area and intended for the growing middle classes settling in the area in the 1880s and 1890s. The large, projecting second-floor gables are timber-framed and supported on brackets.

Next to them is a church which has a strong claim to be Joseph Goddard's masterpiece. The Church of St John the Baptist was built in 1884-85. It is impressive in its scale and in the imposing plainness of its outer walls, achieved by building the supporting buttresses inside where they form dramatic, narrow spaces in the aisles and baptistery. The sweeping

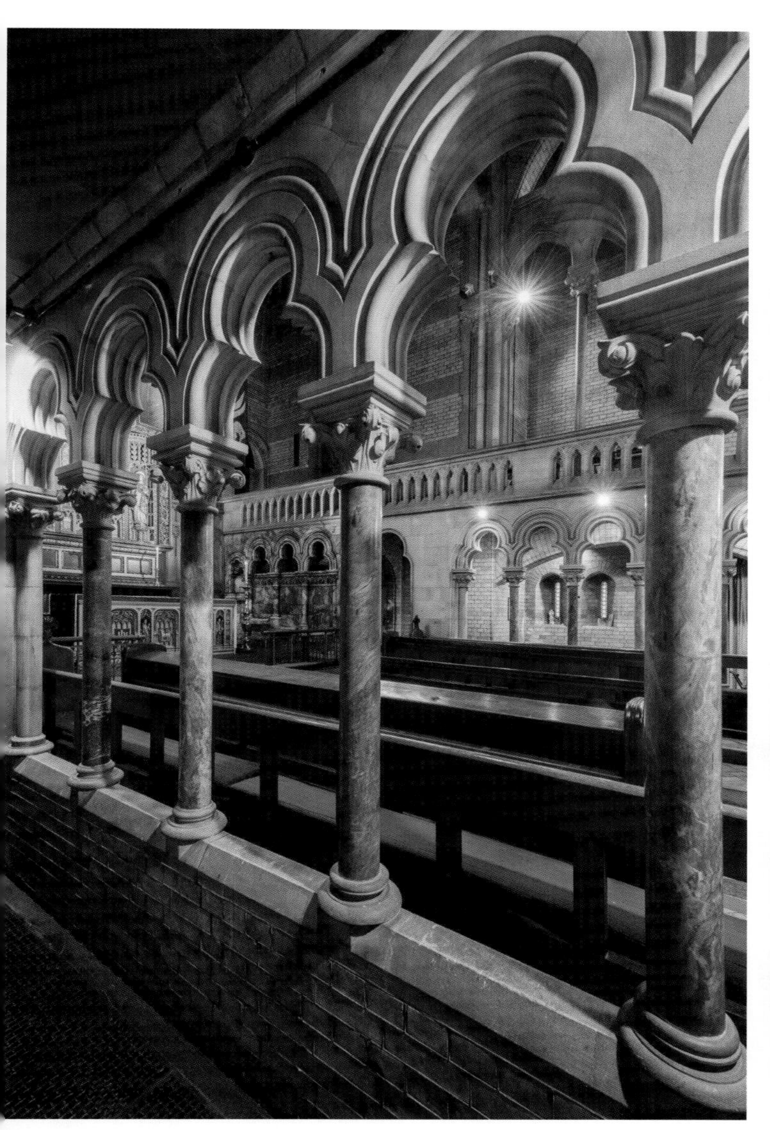

Church of St John the Baptist, Clarendon Park Road

Details of wrought ironwork and (right) stonework, Church of St John the Baptist

red-tiled roof is adorned only by a small, lead-covered Gothic spire. Goddard admired and sketched JL Pearson's Church of St Augustine, Kilburn in London and emulates the arrangement of internal buttresses at St Johns.[99]

The striking landmark of Clarendon Park Congregational Church, built around the same time as St Johns, was built in red Mountsorrel granite rubble and buff sandstone. Its architect James Tait produced a bold and original design with zig-zag tracery in the windows fronting Springfield Road and north German influence in the wide tower at the eastern end.

Springfield Road

Springfield Road

Springfield Road was laid out in 1884 by Isaac Barradale.[100] Its varied mix of building ages, styles and materials, small-scale pattern of development and skylines shaped by gables and chimney stacks typify much of the character of the south-eastern suburbs. Number 2 Springfield Road is a white-stuccoed Classical house from the 1840s or 1850s: the early stages of the development of Stoneygate. Like The Firs, it would have been built among fields and, with its big, spreading cedar trees, looks like a small estate for a country gentleman.

Numbers 4-6, built in about 1900, are further examples of the versatility of the Goddard practice. Here Goddard, Paget and Goddard developed a version of the Queen Anne style of Richard Norman Shaw, a nationally known architect working in this and other styles. Big

4 and 6 Springfield Road

windows form an almost continuous band of glazing on the second floor. Springfield Road continues the established red-brick and red-tile theme with decorative moulded brickwork. A corner turret at number 10 is echoed by a turreted meeting room and chapel in the garden of the Bishop's Lodge, designed by Douglas Smith Stimpson Partnership and built in 1993. Number 25, constructed in 1982-83, echoes its neighbours in materials but is a modern geometrical counterpoint to the buildings around it designed by architect and artist Theo Matoff when he was head of the School of Architecture at Leicester Polytechnic.

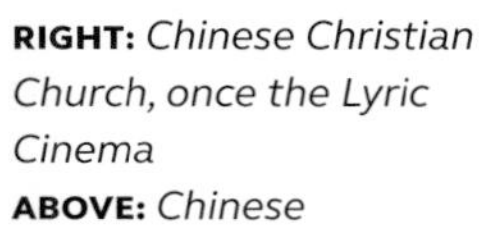

RIGHT: *Chinese Christian Church, once the Lyric Cinema*
ABOVE: *Chinese Christian Church,*
LEFT: *22 Avenue Road*

Clarendon Park Road and Queens Road have a relaxed, cosmopolitan atmosphere with shops, cafés and a varied mix of architectural styles and materials. The big octagonal tower of Clarendon Park Christchurch, built in 1900, forms a striking end-stop to Portland Road. On the opposite side of Clarendon Park Road, the characteristically flamboyant Queen Anne-style Chinese Christian church was originally designed by Arthur Wakerley as a cinema. Nearby at number 70, the Shree Geeta Bhavan Hindu temple and community centre is an adaptation of an early 20th century brick building, including the addition of a columned porch with three tall shikharas.[101]

Number 22 Avenue Road is one of the most notable 20th century houses in Leicester, or for its period in England. Its original owners, Harold and Joan Goddard, had a keen interest in architecture and design particularly of contemporary trends in architecture in Europe and the United States. They commissioned Fello Atkinson and Brenda Walker of James Cubitt and Partners to design the house which was built in 1953-54 at a time of severe

ABOVE AND RIGHT:
Clarendon Park Christchurch

Shree Geeta Bhavan Hindu Temple, Clarendon Park Road

shortage of building materials. From the road, the single-storey house looks like little more than a sheer wall with a garage door. But on the other side the rooms look onto a courtyard garden with a separate garden room built in 1958 when materials were becoming more easily available.

Moving south, Ratcliffe Road has some of the greenest suburban street views in the city. Long property boundaries overhung by mature trees and gentle edges to the street, formed by hedges, railings and timber fences, all give the road a soft and leafy quality. Joseph Goddard designed Knighton Spinneys as his own house and the final expression of his elevation to wealth and social status. Built in 1885, the house has big timber gables facing the road and deep clay-tile roofs. The detail that catches the eye is the gate lodge with its projecting first floor that pushes into views along the road: evidence perhaps that Goddard's aspirations had moved beyond a fine house to a small estate needing a collection of service buildings.

At the junction of Elms Road and Ratcliffe Road, Ernest Gimson built Inglewood for himself in 1892, although he never lived there. Like the White House, its design is simple, meticulous and dramatic. Inglewood is built in subtly patterned red brick with a tall, narrow projecting gable facing Ratcliffe Road. The large roofs, including the long catslide to the front, are among the best examples of Swithland slate roofing in the city.[102] The house has proved comfortable and liveable for generations of owners and has adapted to changing individual needs and lifestyles. There is a sense of hands-on craftsmanship throughout the interior of the house, particularly in the decorative plasterwork with friezes of fruits, vines and flowers.

TOP AND BOTTOM: *Knighton Spinneys*

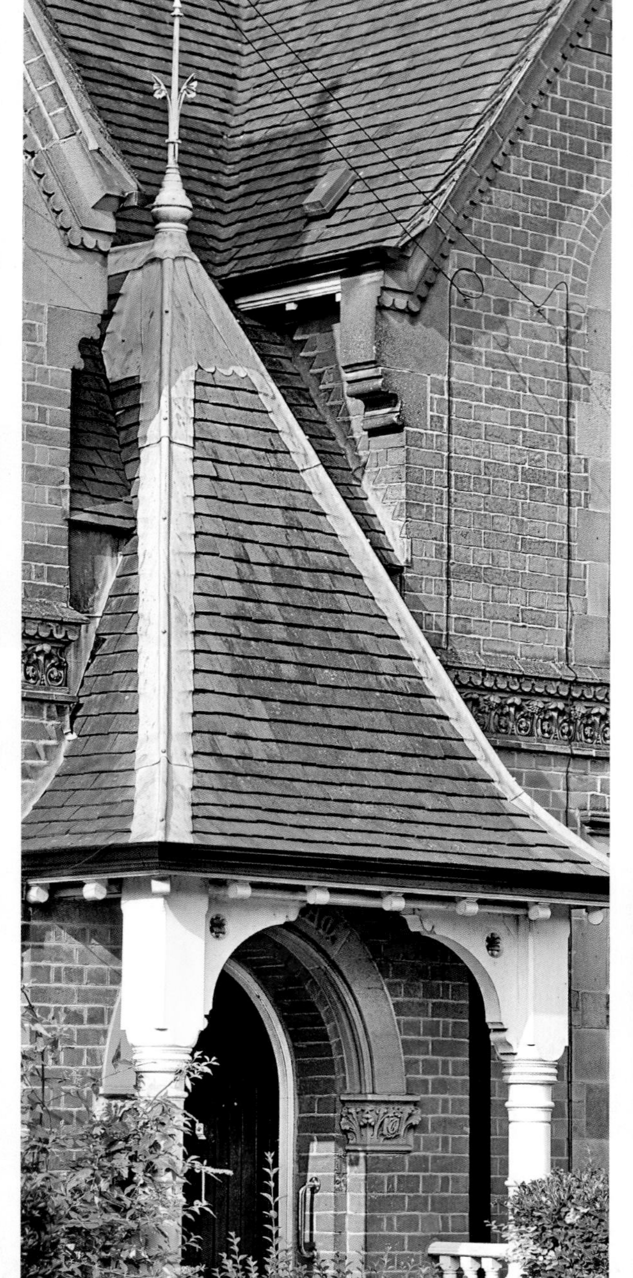

ABOVE AND LEFT: *75 Knighton Drive* **RIGHT:** *Knighton Spinneys, Ratcliffe Road* **ABOVE RIGHT:** *13 Stoneygate Avenue*

LEFT, ABOVE AND RIGHT:
Inglewood

Elms Road leads southwards to the self-contained enclave of South Knighton. Architects and developers who designed large houses, industrial and commercial buildings were also active in laying out streets of terraced houses with local amenities. Shenton and Baker began setting out streets in South Knighton with Sidney Road in 1876, moving on to Knighton Church Road and other streets. Many of the houses were designed by Frank Seale.[103] Although properties vary in size they form a regular pattern of plot sizes, repeated bays, gables and dormers, and decorative details. Hedges and front walls give continuity to the

Suburban street scene, Elms Road

Knighton Church Road

BELOW AND LEFT: *Barron House, London Road and doorway*

street frontages. The area was served by ocal shops and by the Arts and Crafts Church of St Guthlac, built in 1912 as he last design of Stockdale Harrison.

The suburban cross-section continues across London Road at Morland Avenue. Stockdale Harrison laid out the road in 1904 and designed a group of houses towards the western end. The houses are mainly faced in white roughcast render and sparingly decorated but with variety in the design of porches, gables, gutters and downpipes. Large sheets of glass were available by this time (see chapter 9) but windows here have small panes, perhaps seeking to echo the appearance of a country cottage. With the avenue of mature birch trees lining the street they evoke something of the countryside that was built over as the suburbs expanded southwards along London Road.

Chapter fifteen

Arthur Wakerley's Leicester

He was an architect by profession but was also active as a property developer and he set out a clear planning vision for the future of Leicester. Wakerley was a member of Bishop Street Methodist Church and a man of firm moral principle. As a local politician he was for many years a member of the borough then the city corporation and was mayor in 1897-98.[104]

Wakerley's work is particularly evident in the industrial suburb of North Evington and in neighbouring Crown Hills. He began buying up land in the area in 1885 at a time when the fringe of the borough was pock-marked by clay and lime pits supplying building materials to the growing town. It was here that Wakerley developed what he intended as a self-contained industrial settlement, pursued his philanthropic enterprises and built his own home at Crown Hills House.

At the heart of Wakerley's vision for North Evington was the Market Square. It never really succeeded as a working market. The police and fire stations were built in 1899 in a free and lively style, mixing big, triangular gables and a shaped Dutch gable all in red brick with dressings and string courses forming horizontal stripes. The gable ends of the red-brick Market Hall continue the Dutch theme adding a little bit of strapwork in sandstone.[105]

FAR LEFT:
Market Square, North Evington: Market Hall (now a madrasah, 1890s bandstand and square layout
LEFT:
Police Station and Fire Station

The Wakerley Centre, former Blind Work Institute, Gwendolen Road

Wakerley laid out streets around the Market Square and houses and factories were developed: St Saviours Road, east of East Park Road, became a mainly industrial area. He designed a terrace of substantial houses for managers in an Arts and Crafts style at 216–243 East Park Road.

Today North Evington is home to a largely Muslim community. The Market Hall is the Jame'ah Uloomul Qur'an madrasah. What was a factory canteen block in Market Square has for many years been a mosque and in 2008 it was given a distinctly Islamic identity, with intricate applied decoration in a range of materials and a dome and minarets rising high over the terraced streets.

The streets around Gwendolen Road all have Wakerley connections (Gwendolen was Arthur's eldest daughter.) Wakerley developed what amounts to a small village for blind people in this area. He built a terrace on Gwendolen Road in 1897–98 and a community hall nearby in 1906. All these are in Wakerley's typical rosy-red brick with big Dutch gables. The Blind Work Institute of 1921 (now the Wakerley Centre) is a contrast. The architect this time was WH Riley who designed the entrance block in a Tudor style built in golden limestone.

In about 1915, Wakerley built a terrace of houses for blind workers on Gedding Road. He had a house at Gedding in Suffolk and the red pantiled roofs, in a material unusual in Leicester, were perhaps intended to echo the traditional architecture of East Anglia. Each carved stone door surround has a different pattern to help residents find their own home.

Market Hall, former works canteen, converted to a mosque

LEFT AND RIGHT: *Houses in Gwendolen Road for the Wycliffe Institute for the Blind*
BELOW: *Detail of plaque*

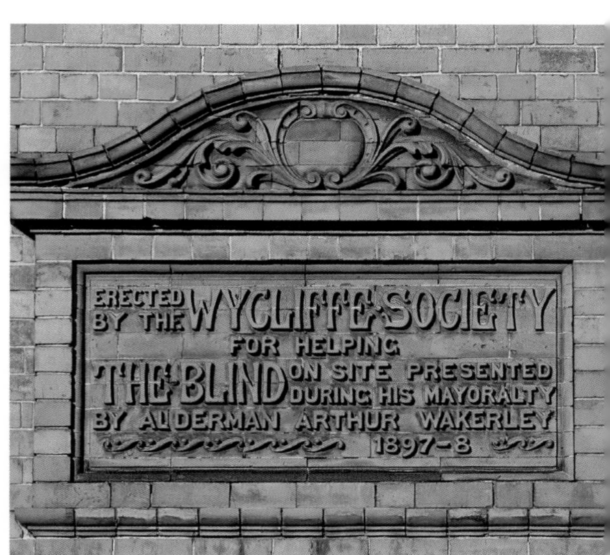

Part of the terrace at 216–243 East Park Road

ABOVE: *Empire Hall, Former St Marks Church*
RIGHT: *The Empire Hall Edie Reid murals*

Sir John Tudor Walters was a Leicester architect and an associate of Wakerley. As MP for Sheffield Brightside, he pioneered detailed standards for new housing after the war in a report of 1917.

Wakerley himself developed a type of house that is his most widespread architectural legacy. The '£299 house' was a response to the post-war housing shortage and to high building costs. The aim of the house was to provide a comfortable home for a reasonable construction cost. There were variations on the basic design but all the houses were built in symmetrical pairs using simple materials and shared services such as gas and water. The designs were adopted in other towns and cities and have proved to be adaptable and resilient. Nearly all of the large stock

£299 houses, Linton Street

of Wakerley houses have been altered but a pair in Linton Street and one in Great Arler Road remain in outwardly unchanged condition.

Wakerley was working at a progressive time in Leicester's history. Another major figure was the Christian Socialist vicar of St Marks Church in Belgrave Gate, Canon F Lewis Donaldson. The church itself is remarkable as a leading work of the architect Ewan Christian in a French Gothic style faced in red Charnwood granite (now converted to the Empire function venue). During Donaldson's time as vicar of St Marks, from 1896 to 1918, the church was expanded and a series of huge mural paintings was commissioned for the chancel apse by the Scottish painter James Edie Reid, depicting the Triumph and Travails of Labour.[106, 107]

Leicestershire Guild for the Disabled, now Hindu temple, Colton Street

View from Keyham Lane, Humberstone

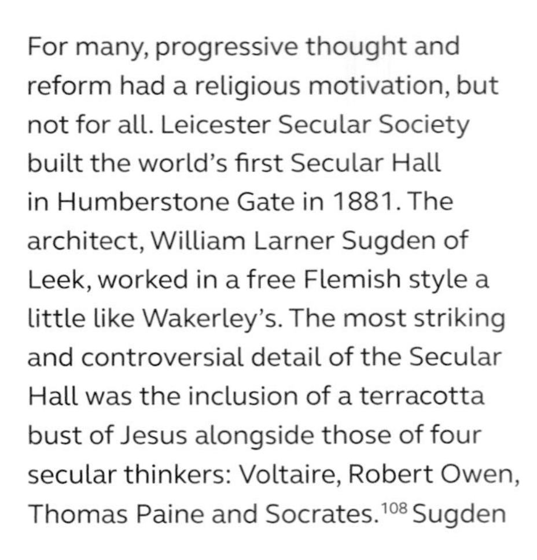

For many, progressive thought and reform had a religious motivation, but not for all. Leicester Secular Society built the world's first Secular Hall in Humberstone Gate in 1881. The architect, William Larner Sugden of Leek, worked in a free Flemish style a little like Wakerley's. The most striking and controversial detail of the Secular Hall was the inclusion of a terracotta bust of Jesus alongside those of four secular thinkers: Voltaire, Robert Owen, Thomas Paine and Socrates.[108] Sugden knew William Morris, the writer, designer, conservationist and, later in his life, socialist. It was meeting Morris when he spoke at the Secular Hall in 1884 that inspired the young Ernest Gimson to develop his own ideas about the socially reforming aspects of design.

The Anchor Boot and Shoe factory in Asfordby Street, North Evington, a cooperative enterprise, developed an initiative to provide housing for its workers. Anchor Tenants bought land at Keyham Lane, Humberstone, to develop a garden suburb. Begun in 1908, the settlement was designed by Raymond Unwin, one of the architects of Letchworth Garden City and a leading figure in the Garden City movement.

In an echo of Wakerley's work for the blind, AE Sawday (or perhaps Ralph Bedingfield in Sawday's office) designed a pioneering building in an Arts and Crafts style in Colton Street for what became the Leicestershire Guild for the

Gateway illustrating Garden City heritage, Humberstone

Disabled. The communal hall, workshops (now demolished) and offices were specially adapted for use by disabled people. The building is now used by a Hindu community as Shri Shirdi Sai Baba temple.

Others had a less direct impact on Leicester's architectural character but were nevertheless influential in improving the borough, some in ways that made a national impact. Benjamin Fletcher was headmaster of the Leicester Municipal School of Art from 1900 to 1920 and was particularly interested in art and design education in Germany and Austria. He developed courses at Leicester linking design and industrial production. Fletcher's friend and collaborator Harry Hardy Peach, founder of the Dryad Company, shared these interests and also campaigned for civic improvements such as the provision of bus shelters, hygienic public toilets, better design of shopfronts and the laying-out of what is now Castle Gardens as a memorial to the dead of the First World War.

This remarkable group of people also included Harry Simpson Gee and his son Percy Gee of the Stead and Simpson shoe company who funded the foundation of a university college: the institution that was to become the University of Leicester.

FROM LEFT TO RIGHT: *Secular Hall, Humberstone Gate: exterior, window in the main hall, bust of Voltaire, exterior of building, Voltaire decorative facade, detail of lamp over main entrance*

Market Street

SECTION FOUR

20TH CENTURY CITY

The newly honoured City of Leicester commemorated the loss of its citizens in war with a sombre, magnificent memorial. The 1920s and 1930s were generally good years for the city and its commercial, industrial and civic confidence were expressed in buildings in a range of old and new materials and by innovative architectural styles.

Chapter sixteen

1919

1919 was a pivotal year in world history and a crucial year for Leicester. On 10 June that year King George V visited Leicester and knighted Jonathan North at De Montfort Hall in recognition of his leadership of the borough as mayor during the years of the First World War. A month later a royal charter was granted conferring the title 'City of Leicester'.[109]

Victoria Park was laid out in 1883 on the site of the town's racecourse. The elements of the design are simple: avenues of trees divide large areas of grass used for sports, big events and informal recreation. The park is airy and spacious but buildings and buzzing traffic around the edges give Victoria Park a decidedly urban setting.

The park was chosen as the site of the city's war memorial and Leicester commissioned the best available architect, Sir Edwin Lutyens, to design a profoundly serious structure and one of Leicester's finest buildings. Lutyens designed memorials in Delhi and on the Somme battlefield as well as the Cenotaph in London. Leicester's memorial, the Arch of Remembrance, was built in concrete and clad in Portland stone with stone flags in the archway and it stands comparison with Lutyens's other work. The open expanse of thepark provides a setting in which the monumental quality of the memorial can be seen and felt; the lofty arch seems to embrace the sky and views of the city.

The memorial, dedicated in 1925, commemorates the 12,000 men and women from Leicestershire who died in the First World War as well as others who served or "patiently endured".[110] A more modest monument nearby in Welford Road Cemetery gives a hint of the nature of some of the individual stories behind that harrowing total. Eight Belgian soldiers who died in Leicester are recorded, one simply as *inconnu* 'unknown', a quiet commemoration of a young man who died far from home in the first months of the war without record of his name.[111]

LEFT: *Victoria Park* **ABOVE:** *Lodges and gates at park entrance on London Road*
BELOW: *Arch of Remembrance, Peace Walk with gates and gate piers to University Road*

MCM
XLV

Leicester's war memorial, the Arch of Remembrance, from north-east

LEFT: *De Montfort Hall, Concerto sculpture by John Sidney Hall* **ABOVE:** *De Montfort Hall interior*

Sir Jonathan North's wife, Kate Eliza, died in 1930 and North commemorated her by funding a programme of improvements to the setting of the war memorial and to the park.[112] Once again Lutyens was commissioned. The original square enclosure to the memorial was replaced by the present circle with Greek gatepiers in Portland stone and iron railings. The processional route to University Road, originally called War Memorial Approach but renamed Peace Walk in 1981, was enhanced by a screen of six Portland stone gatepiers topped by flaming urns and superbly-made wrought-iron gates, overthrow and railings.

These works were carried out between 1931 and 1933 and the improvements to the park continued up to 1935. The pair of gate-lodges on London Road illustrate Lutyens's free and inventive classical style typified by quoins, normally indicating a corner or division, set on a flat wall. The lodges are faced in Portland stone and stucco lined to imitate stonework. The gates echo those on University Road but here the blacksmith made an even finer set of gates, overthrow and railings.

De Montfort Hall was built in 1913 to the design of Shirley Harrison, the son of Stockdale Harrison. The present configuration of the hall was the result of a major programme of conversion and extension carried out by the city council between 1993 and 1994.

The spare classical exterior and internal space, decorated mainly by a series of giant scrolled brackets, provides an elegant arena which has hosted many of the greatest names of pop and classical music, and has staged graduation ceremonies, remembrance services and community celebrations. The De Montfort Hall organ was made by the Leicester company Stephen Taylor and Son. It was played at a reopening recital in 1998 after repair by Richard Young, son of the last of Taylor's apprentices.[113]

LEFT: *Church of St James the Greater, London Road, interior*

Land to build a church on the north side of the park was donated in 1864 and a temporary forerunner of the Church of St James the Greater was built on the site. Later Henry Langton Goddard was commissioned to design a permanent church. His first design was Gothic but at the suggestion of the Bishop of Peterborough, whose diocese then included Leicester, Goddard travelled to Italy to study several churches there. The chief infuence on the Italian-inspired

ABOVE: *Church of St James the Greater, elevation to London Road*

ABOVE TOP: *Burmantofts terracotta detail*
ABOVE: *Detail of internal arcade*

ABOVE: *Statue of St James the Greater*

design that resulted was the cathedral at Torcello in the Venice Lagoon. This was the inspiration for the round-arched early-Christian style that gives St James its graceful, serene interior. Burmantofts made the prolific terracotta angels in the church which featured in the company's catalogue in 1902. The baroque front facing the park was completed in 1914.

The area between the London Road park lodges and the war memorial was for many years filled by car parking and sports facilities. In 2016 an avenue was laid out which improves access and visibility between the set of buildings by Sir Edwin Lutyens, and provides a public space that extends the pedestrian promenade of New Walk into the park.

Victoria Park combines the solemnity of the war memorial with the enjoyment and relaxation of informal football games and the cricket matches that take place, boundary to boundary, on summer evenings. It is a venue for circuses and concerts and a place for Eid celebrations, the Caribbean Carnival, Pride festivities and the Jewish Hanukkah Menorah. The park is a popular space for recreation, remembrance and the celebration of Leicester's multiple identities.

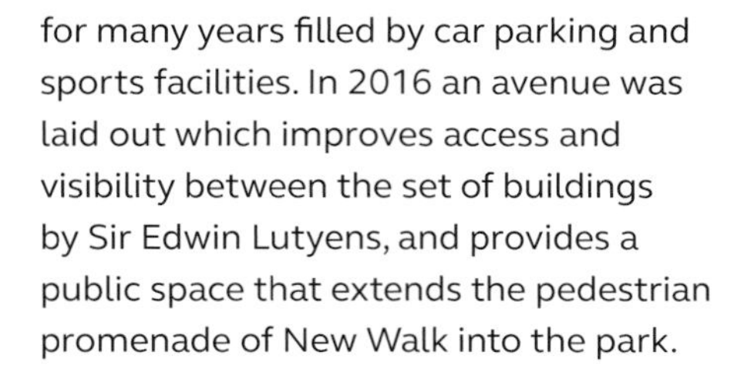

16 May 2016: Leicester City Football Club. Premier League Victory Parade. Thousands gather to celebrate at Victoria Park

Chapter seventeen

Homes for the 20th century city

The end of the First World War brought a spirit of reform and progress but also a serious housing shortage, made worse by the devastating effect of the war on the workforce and by a steep rise in building costs.

The corporation bought land in Braunstone, outside Leicester's administrative boundary until 1935, to cope with the demand for new housing for rent. A growing bus network connected residents to what initially seemed to many to be a distant city. The ideas of the garden city movement, seen for example at Humberstone: individual houses with gardens, trees, open spaces and an element of community living, were highly influential (see chapter 15).

The corporation, with its architect James Simpson Fyfe, started to build in South Braunstone in 1927 to 1928. The showpiece was the prominent crescent at 317–335 Narborough Road. The houses form a curved group of cottages, three with big timber-framed gables, set back from the main road with maturing trees on the green space. The houses have been altered but much of the original sense of Fyfe's design remains.

Shops, schools and churches were built to support the life of the community.

Gooding Avenue, on the east side of Braunstone Park, has a variety of house types including some for older people and open views into the park. The shape of the individual houses, their layout, gardens and the spacious overall environment have proved resilient despite changes to nearly all the individual houses.

In the years from the late 1990s government initiatives have provided a new health centre and the relocation of the city's main swimming pool to Braunstone as part of a new leisure centre.

FAR LEFT AND MIDDLE: *317–335 Narborough Road* **RIGHT:** *Gooding Avenue*

Braunstone Park from Gooding Avenue

Westfield Road

Western Park is a different sort of suburb but one that also shows the influence of the garden city movement, not least in taking the name of Letchworth Garden City in Hertfordshire for its main spine road. Western Park was built on land sloping down from Glenfield Road to Hinckley Road. Letchworth Road is a tree-lined avenue dipping to the east affording views of the city centre. Western Park was developed as a residential estate from about 1900 and John Tudor Walters (see chapter 15) was active as an architect and developer.

The principal landmark is St Annes Church, designed by Arthur Bryan and built in 1934. The main material is a brownish brick with stone tracery in the windows in the Decorated Gothic style. The church was never completed as originally intended (the west end is built in a non-matching brick intended to be temporary) but its bold, lofty composition and hilltop location make St Annes an imposing architectural centrepiece to Western Park.

St Annes Church, Letchworth Road

Sunnycroft Road

Letchworth Road

Houses vary in type and size. An unusual group in Sunnycroft Road, for example, have timbered gables and central front doors. Houses in Letchworth Road form an impressive sequence built for business and professional people. Their style is still influenced by the Arts and Crafts movement but in inventive ways, often incorporating garages, by now a requirement for well-heeled owners. Summer Hill, like many other houses in the area, was designed by Ralph Waldo Bedingfield. Built in 1906, it combines much of the prevailing style and many of the materials typical of Western Park: long roof slopes, warm red brick and red clay tiles used for roofing or hung vertically as a wall covering.

Other houses are rendered in white-painted stucco. The most striking example is Green Gables on Westhill Road, built in the 1930s. The white outer walls, green glazed pantile roof, horizontal metal windows and an arched front door set in an outwardly splayed centre bay give the house a sunny, seaside appearance that would not be out of place in the Mediterranean or in southern California.

On Westfield Road, one example among thousands represents the suburban semi-detached house. Built in huge numbers by local authorities and private developers in streets, crescents and cul-de-sacs, the semi was seen as an improvement on terraces for large-scale housing. Derided by architectural purists as the epitome of suburban dullness, the semi has survived all the condescension to become one of the most popular and successful house types ever built.

Letchworth Road

Letchworth Road

Letchworth Road

Chapter eighteen
Style and function

Within a mixed local economy, Leicester firms did well betweeen 1919 and 1939. The city was far from immune to national and international economic turbulence, but in 1936 the League of Nations found that, on the basis of household income, Leicester was the second most prosperous city in Europe.[114] Some of this wealth was spent on buildings by private companies and by the corporation or funded through philanthropy.

The arrival of modern architectural ideas from Europe and the United States and the increasing use of structures built around concrete or steel frames led increasingly to a rectilinear and unadorned style that was to become more dominant after the Second World War. Materials could be sourced nationally so the distinctiveness provided by a range of local materials was reduced. The Critall Company of Essex produced windows with frames of ribbon-like steel strips. These were sold in Leicester through a local branch and were widely used in the city. Other new materials came onto the market, including new types of glass.

Local services expanded. Great steel gas holders were built on Aylestone Meadows in the 1930s and the period also saw the appearance of the familiar tapered forms of electricity pylons and of carefully detailed brick substations. Tram, and then bus networks expanded, producing stylish little Art Deco shelters designed for Critall by WK Bedingfield and Percy Herbert Grundy at points around the city, including Humberstone Park and Western Park.

In some ways the strangest building of this period was the General Accident Fire and Life offices in Wellington Street, a five-storey building whose big timber-framed prow on a sandstone base closes the southward view along Market Street. Built in 1931–32 to the design of architects GPK Young and Son of Perth, it seems to reflect a vision of the Midlands closer to the timber buildings of Chester or Shrewsbury than to red-brick Leicester.

ABOVE AND LEFT:
Bus Shelter, Western Boulevard

Former General Accident Fire and Life offices, Wellington Street

ABOVE: *Fire Station, Lancaster Road* **BELOW LEFT:** *Fire Station houses* **BELOW:** *Detail of wyvern and lamp*

The Fire Station on Lancaster Road was designed by AE and T Sawday and built in 1925–27. It combines a steel-framed structure with a simplified Georgian style, the engine bays forming an arcade along the ground-floor frontage. The Fire Station was a self-contained community with firefighters living in cottages clustered around the station.

Wyggeston Girls' Grammar School is a more ambitious building but still in a spare classical style built in brick with an impressive front entrance in Portland stone. Opened in 1928, the school was

ABOVE: *Regent College (Former Wyggeston Girls' Grammar School)* **BELOW LEFT:** *Regent College, assembly hall (now subdivided)* **BELOW RIGHT:** *Regent College, Wyggeston coat of arms*

generously endowed by Sir Jonathan North. The architects, Symington Prince and Pike, was a practice which made a significant mark on Leicester in this period. Inside, the building has fine examples of architectural craftsmanship in the form of bookshelves, fittings and plasterwork. The school was built around two courtyards with access originally governed by rules restricting some areas to teachers and sixth-formers.[115] Today, as Regent College, it is a dynamic place providing sixth-form education to a diverse range of students.

The competition to design Saffron Hill Cemetery was won by a leading park designer of the early 20th century, Thomas Mawson and Son of Lancaster and Windermere. The cemetery, opened in 1931, is the most significant public space of this period in Leicester. Its layout is based on two carriage drives from the entrance gates to the chapels with enclosures for burials on either side. Intended as open lawns uncluttered by bulky monuments.' Prentice Mawson designed the buildings.

The beautiful chapel, with its bell tower rising above the trees, is in a simplified Romanesque style with a northern Italian character. Inside is a white, calm and consoling space for burial services. In 1985 Leicester City Council became the first in Europe to provide a *janazgah*, a prayer house for the Muslim burial rite, built close to the chapel.

Art Deco is a style of architecture and decorative art that broke away from the sinuous curves of Art Nouveau in favour of geometrical patterns, especially chevrons, abstract forms and motifs, some derived from the popular interest in ancient Egyptian artefacts.

These elements are brought together by Percy Grundy in a building for Goddards' Silver Polish Company, now Berkeley Burke House, built in 1932 in Nelson Street. The central bays fronting Nelson Street and Regent Street are faced with panels of Crittall glazing hung on an internal frame as curtain walling between bays of mottled brick and honey coloured sandstone.[116] Decoration includes chevrons, waves and starbursts as well as abstract stone finials on the ends of the frontage to Nelson Street. Nearby, Grundy designed a block of shops on the corner of London Road and Nelson Street, forming a small Art Deco street scene.

ABOVE AND BELOW: *Berkeley Burke House, leadwork detail with chevron and wave decoration*

Saffron Hill Cemetery, chapel

Pork Pie Library and Community Centre

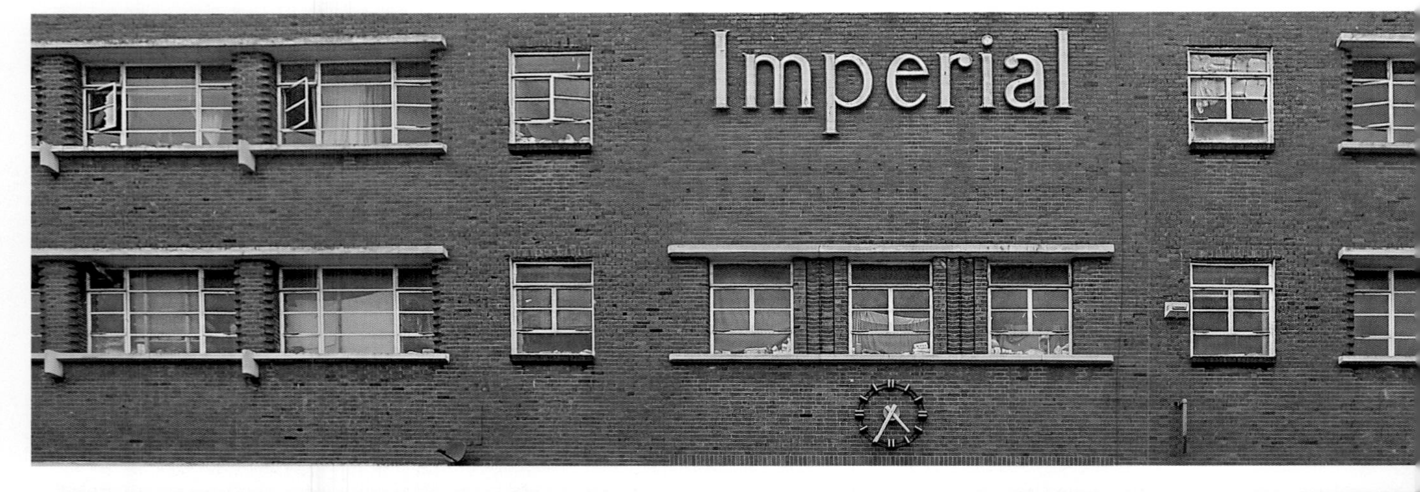

Former Imperial Typewriters Building, East Park Road

In 1936, Pick Everard Keay and Gimson won an award from the Royal Institute of British Architects (RIBA) for their factory for Imperial Typewriters in East Park Road. It is austere and utilitarian in comparison with the more playful Art Deco style of other buildings in this chapter. The front is built in dark-red and blue brick with horizontal steel-framed windows and simple decoration in the balcony railing and clock on the centre bay. At the back, the building is fully glazed to provide light to the factory floors.

The two circular libraries, West Humberstone in St Barnabas Road and Southfields on Attlee Way, both built in 1937–39, are among the most prominent and popular buildings by Symington Prince and Pike. The former Southfields Library, now known as Pork Pie Library and Community centre, is the more elaborate composition with a series of drums building up to the central 'Pork Pie' tower, containing the reading room. The design reflects that of Stockholm Library from 1928 and the London Underground stations on the Piccadilly Line, particularly the circular entrance hall of Arnos Grove station of 1932.[117] Perhaps Maurice Pike was also influenced by his collection of tobacco tins which he used to experiment with forms for the libraries.[118]

Southfields Library is beautifully built in buff handmade brick. Attention to detail extends to the interior parquet floor and fitted bookshelves and to the suggestion of Art Deco detail in the external railings Tall Crittall windows make the reading room light and spacious and the side rooms provide spaces for classes and community gatherings.

Pork Pie Library and Community Centre, interior of reading room

Internal lettering and finishes

128–132 Granby Street, 1933

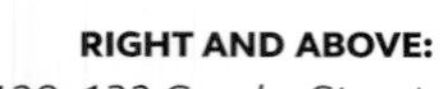

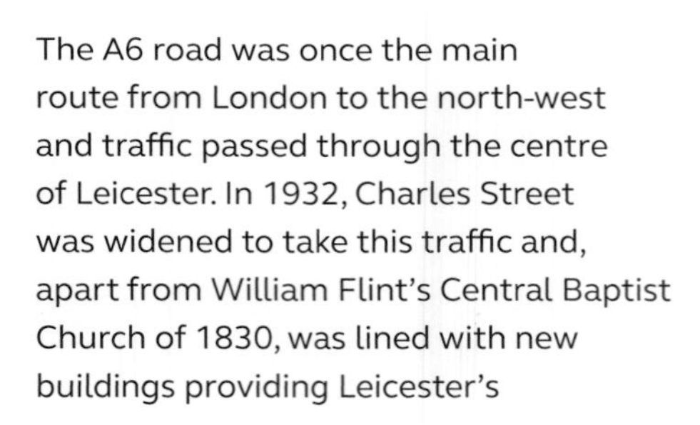

RIGHT AND ABOVE:
128–132 Granby Street, detail of pilaster capital

The A6 road was once the main route from London to the north-west and traffic passed through the centre of Leicester. In 1932, Charles Street was widened to take this traffic and, apart from William Flint's Central Baptist Church of 1830, was lined with new buildings providing Leicester's most complete street scene of the period.

Portland stone was favoured for civic and commercial buildings and there are four Portland landmarks along the new highway. The northbound driver would have swung sharp right by 128-132 Granby Street (now Blunts Shoes) on a prominent corner. Symington Prince and Pike's building of 1933 is basically Classical in style but treated in a cheerful, free Art Deco manner, especially in the stylised design of the Corinthian pilaster capitals.

Former police station, Colton Square

The former police station, now the centrepiece of the Colton Square office development, was designed by Noel Hill, then working as an architect for the corporation.

The arched central entrance and chief constable's office with its doors and balcony set in a big expanse of Portland ashlar look appropriately serious and institutional. Kay Bee House at 118 Charles Street is a commercial building which won an RIBA award for Symington Prince and Pike in 1933. The Portland frontage is in a simplified classical style but with a hint of Art Deco in the wavy lines cast into the metal panels between the windows.

Lewis's Tower, Humberstone Gate

It was as the motorist bore right at the Rutland Street junction that he would have encountered the most impressive of Leicester's new Portland landmarks. Liverpool architects Barnish and Silcock (Leonard Barnish and H Spencer Silcock) won a competition to design new municipal offices for Leicester which were opened in 1938. The design is spare and unadorned and may have been influenced by certain continental European buildings of the time.

Municipal offices had an eventful life and parts have been used as an electricity showroom, a bank, a nuclear bunker and as a snooker hall run by Leicester sporting hero Willie Thorne. In 2014 the building returned to full civic use as the council's new headquarters, following a conversion scheme designed by Franklin Ellis Architects. Among the evidence of past uses, three futuristic paintings promoting the benefits of electricity now hang in the theatre where appliances were once demonstrated to eager buyers.

Traffic controls at the busy junction with Humberstone Gate would have given the northbound driver time to glance left at the sleek and modern Portland stone tower of the new Lewis's department store, built in 1935–36 originally as part of a bigger composition in the same stone.

ABOVE: *City Hall, former Municipal Offices, Charles Street*
BELOW: *City Hall, staircase* **MIDDLE BELOW:** *City Hall, mural paintings in electricity demonstration theatre*
RIGHT BELOW: *City Hall, entrance hall*

Kingstone Store, Belgrave Gate

Temple Buildings, dated 1934 and now occupied by Limz Designs, is an elaborate example of the Art Deco style applied to an industrial building. The main material is red brick decorated with recessed bands and curved buttresses but the design also includes an elaborate stone and concrete doorway and glass panels of chevrons in red, white and blue on a pink background. The Kingstone store of 1937 pointed the way to architecture of the years after 1945. Sir Charles Keene, the owner of Kingstone, commissioned Australian architect Raymond McGrath to design the store. McGrath's style was simple and uncluttered. He was interested in the use of glass in architecture and the design for Kingstone used sheets of pink Vitrolite for cladding the front elevation and, originally, the elevation to Bedford Street. Vitrolite was an opaque coloured glass product which was widely used in the 1930s, particularly for shopfronts and interior design. Kingstone was the first building in which it was used without fixing bars for the vertical joints. Pink Vitrolite is unobtainable now and some broken panels were pieced-in during the 1990s with a substitute material.[119]

Leicester's architecture in the years between 1919 and 1939 was varied, looked outward for its influences and contributed to making a better city for Leicester people. The period of prosperity that the city enjoyed in those years left some outstanding and adaptable buildings that continue to be used and enjoyed.

Temple Buildings, Temple Road, Evington

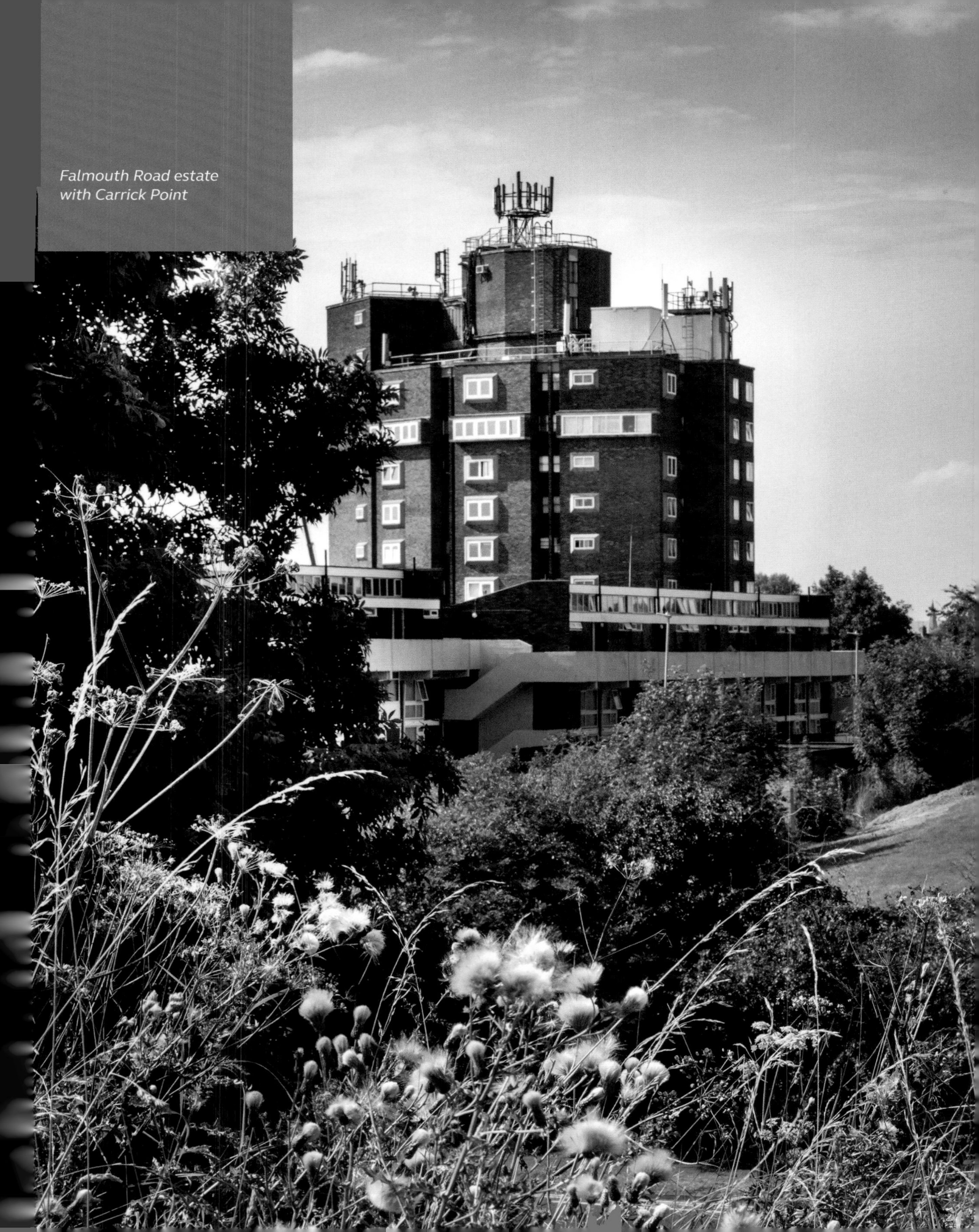

Falmouth Road estate with Carrick Point

SECTION FIVE

MODERN CITY

The city centre was changed by road building and large scale commercial development and outer areas saw rapid urban expansion. The city's universities developed impressive campuses and environmental concerns gave Leicester's parks, open spaces and riverside a new importance. New communities arriving in the city began to establish characteristic buildings and street scenes that give Leicester much of its present distinctiveness.

Chapter nineteen

Expansion

After the Second World War, growth in population and the need to replace slum housing led to a revival of the pre-war house building programme by the corporation, with the development of estates in areas such as New Parks, Thurnby Lodge, Stocking Farm and Eyres Monsell. Private developers, both local and national firms, were also building semi-detached and detached houses in volume in the suburbs. Later, housing associations became important housing providers.

The local distinctiveness of building materials had been eroded by 1945 but local companies such as Ibstock, which began by using clay from the Leicestershire coal measures, and Charnwood Brick offered products comparable with the characteristic Leicester red brick.

The corporation bought the Evington House Estate in 1947 and Evington Park was opened in

FAR LEFT: *Evington House and Evington Park* **MIDDLE LEFT:** *Cordery Avenue, Evington*
TOP LEFT AND RIGHT: *Aldgate Avenue, Evington* **ABOVE:** *Cordery Avenue, Evington*

the following year. The housing development around Cordery Road and Aldgate Avenue, built in the early 1950s, retained a number of the fine parkland trees which still give this area its special character. The estate echoes developments of the same time in the new towns in protecting established trees and building mixed housing types around greens and play areas connected to continuous streets.

Building materials were in short supply so the houses are faced in a machine-made red brick or in painted render and have brown concrete-tile roofs. The area has matured into a pleasant estate wrapping around two sides of the park. The small groups of bungalows form well-defined corners or nestle below the big mature trees.

Mayflower Primary School, Evington Drive

Linden Primary School, Headland Road

The growing communities needed primary schools. In the Evington area Whitehall, Linden and Mayflower schools were all built in the early 1950s in a light-orange brick and in a common style: single-storey and with big steel-framed windows to let lots of light into the classrooms.

The Roman Catholic Church has been a patron of good church architecture and St Josephs Church, at the junction of Uppingham Road and Goodwood Road, is a fine example. Built in 1967–68 to the design of Thomas Wilson of Oakham, the church combines a circular worship area with a soaring, tapered 24 metre-high bell tower faced in honey-coloured quartzite tiles. The design uses modern construction to provide an imposing landmark in the suburban landscape.

On the far west side of the city the Church of England built St Aidans Church in 1959 to serve New Parks and neighbouring areas. It is a much simpler design than St Josephs, with an open concrete framed tower and a tiled mural illustrating the life of St Aidan. Its architects, Basil Spence and Partners, also designed Coventry Cathedral.

St Aidans Church, New Parks, mosaic mural illustrating the life of St Aidan

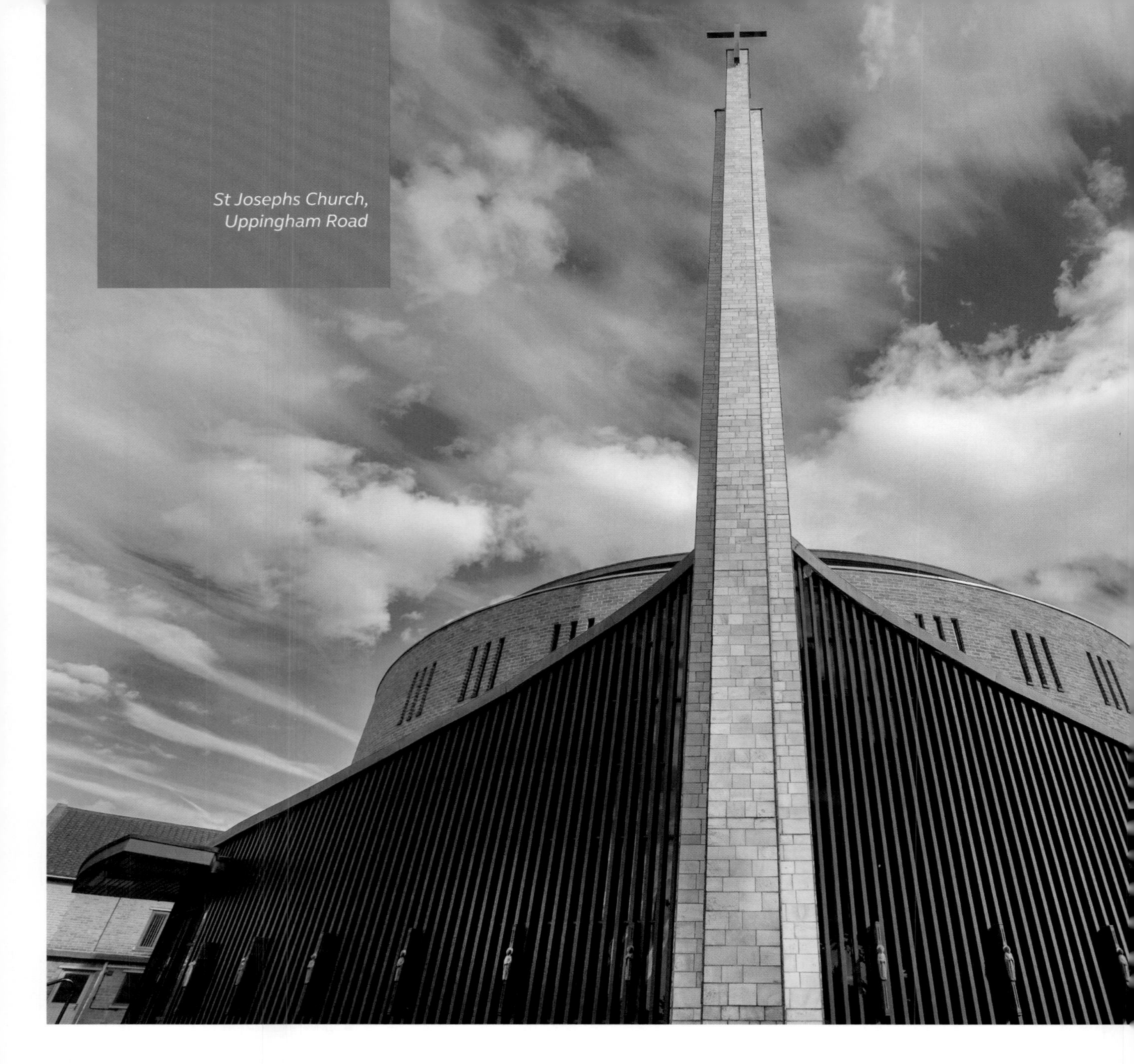

St Josephs Church, Uppingham Road

The Leicester Co-ownership Housing Society commissioned Douglas Smith Stimson Partnership to design the Falmouth Road estate in Evington in the early 1970s. The plan mixed houses in short terraces, four-storey flats and a 14-storey tower block in a scheme which still has an architectural coherence that sets it apart from the surrounding suburbs, helped by now mature planting.

The construction of the tower, Carrick Point, was notable. Instead of a steel or concrete frame the brickwork itself supports the structure, helped by the many facets and recesses in the plan.

In 1967 Konrad Smigielski as city planning officer, drew up a plan for a new town for 40,000 people on council-owned land at Beaumont Leys (see chapter 13). The plan was a strong and modern architectural vision with much of the population living in flats. A monorail would have linked the new town with the city centre. A start was made on a pilot area south of Krefeld Way. But by the 1970s, by which time John Dean was city planning officer, much had changed and it was clear that most people preferred a house

ABOVE: *Falmouth Road Estate*
RIGHT: *Krefeld Way*

with a garden. Smigielski's bold design gave way to a more pragmatic plan for a smaller target population. Existing landscape features and the handful of older buildings were retained.

The council aimed to encourage a range of different housing designs and types and this was at least partly successful. In the pilot area the range of styles was generally quite limited, although there were variations in layout and links to spaces and trees. Houses were mostly faced in brick or render with concrete roof tiles.

Halley Close

Halley Close

To the north of Krefeld Way there was greater variety. In 1986 De Montfort Housing Society opened Halley Close. The architect, John Middleton designed the scheme to echo the best features of a Leicestershire village street, carefully mixing materials and house types within a restricted budget. At Brackenfield Chase, in the north of the development area, Barry Beesley Design devised a scheme in 1988 for Balfour Beatty that also used traditional Leicestershire building materials, including thatch for roofing on some of the houses, in this case built for owner-occupiers. Both schemes are a long way from Smigielski's original idea but succeed on their own terms in creating distinctive places.

Beaumont Leys was intended to be a self-contained town with a range of land uses. The Bursom Industrial Estate is the biggest of the employment area dominated by big factory buildings, many clad in sheet steel. In the first industrial area at Boston Road the units are mostly smaller and offer greater scope for architectural expression within a range of colours specified by the council. In 1971-74 Douglas Smith Stimson Partnership designed an office and industrial building for Monarch Knitting Machinery (UK) Ltd with a long, sleek front building in buff brick and dark brown steel cladding. The strong profile is enhanced by the treatment of the firm's name and logo which are integrated into the architecture using red, deep-profile blocks. A building designed by Marsh Grochowski Architects nearby in Boston Road, built in about 2000, uses a similar buff brick and the front windows are set back behind a sequence of brick columns. This provides shading in a building built to high environmental standards and presents an elegant frontage to the road.[120]

Monarch factory and offices, Boston Road

The proposed self-contained settlement of Ashton Green with views of Bradgate Park

The Beaumont Centre provides shopping and facilities for the local community. In the first phase, built in 1983–84, the shops were grouped around a square and a market with the angular form of Christ the King Ecumenical Centre nearby. A later phase, in yellowish buff brick with a naturally-lit arched mall, was added in around 2000.

What was originally intended as a single town has in reality become several neighbourhoods. The next phase, on the land between the development north of Bennion Road and Brackenfield Chase, is proposed to be the self-contained settlement of Ashton Green, to be built to reflect current concerns for environmental protection and sustainability. It is the landscape, especially the nearby skyline of Charnwood Forest, that will give a common thread to the various elements of this north-western part of the city and to the changing values that have shaped it.

Brackenfield Chase

Chapter twenty

The modern centre

Writing in 1957, the landscape historian WG Hoskins, who spent over 20 years in Leicester, described the city as having 'a small town homeliness' and wrote of a 'delightful Betjeman town'.[121] Much of the town Hoskins knew remains but, even as he was writing, changes were planned. Car parks, shopping malls, buildings with large floor areas and roads all caused the loss of much of the small-scale pattern inherited from the medieval burgage plots.

The building of the inner ring road, beginning with Vaughan Way in 1958 and Burleys Way in 1962, helped to retain the central historical core of the city and later enabled some streets to be converted to pedestrian use. But the cost was huge: communities like St Matthews were severed from the city centre and much of the sense and continuity of the western side of the core was lost. The Guildhall and cathedral area, the castle precinct and Jewry Wall and St Nicholas had been linked by a continuous street pattern but became detached enclaves separated by busy roads. The inner ring road would have imposed a cost whichever route was chosen but extensive damage to a historic city that had survived the Second World War largely intact was a heavy price to pay.

Vaughan Way and Burleys Way, linking to the north with St Matthews Way and St Georges Way, still form the main artery carrying traffic to the west and north of the city centre. The roads form a continuous corridor with variations in level through Southgates Underpass and over the curved deck of Burleys Flyover, built in 1970. Tree planting has created something of the sense of a boulevard in the section alongside St Margarets Bus Station. Burleys Way footbridge, its deck supported in Y-shaped concrete piers, direction signs in standard Transport font, the bold patterns of road markings and the textures of concrete and granite setts give some elements of grain and visual quality to the inner ring road.

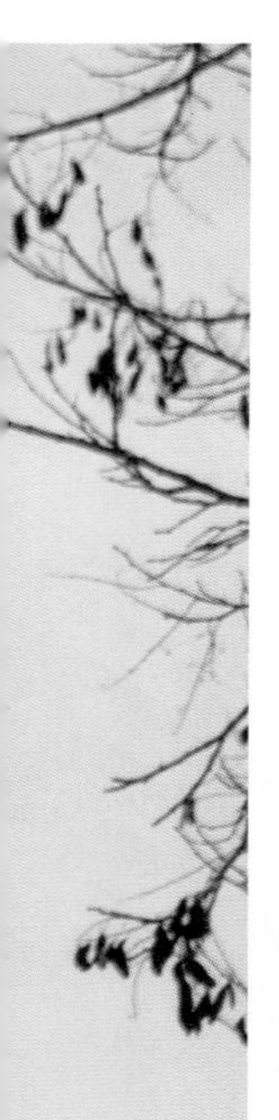

ABOVE FAR LEFT: *Sculpture by Hubert Dalwood*
ABOVE: *Sculpture on Burleys Flyover*

Burleys Flyover

Cardinal Telephone Exchange. In the foreground: Spa Place

Leicester never wholeheartedly adopted tall buildings, though there have been some proposals that were never built and some tall blocks of flats have been demolished. But tall buildings nevertheless form landmarks in distant views and within the city centre.

The oldest of the tall buildings in the city centre is probably the best.

From left to right: St Georges Tower, former Postal Headquarters. Elizabeth House, London Road / Charles Street

The Cardinal Telephone Exchange in Humberstone Gate was built in 1966-67 by the Post Office. The building mainly contains machinery and the exterior appearance is formed by vertical metal and concrete ribs and blue cement panels rather than glass. The 84-metre high tower forms a sheer and elegant gateway to Humberstone Gate. It is also a nesting site for urban peregrines, a once rare species of falcon that can now be glimpsed in the sky over the city.

The group of buildings around the railway station is the nearest that the city came to a coherent cluster of tall commercial buildings.[122]

The main collection of tall buildings is around the transport hub of the railway station. In 1971–72 the Post Office built a big grey concrete and glass office tower that formed an impressive stop at the southern end of Charles Street. The building was converted from about 2003 to a hotel with office and residential use as St Georges Tower. It was painted blue with some window panels picked out in other bright colours.

The change of colour fitted in with some of the buildings around it. Of the cluster of tall buildings, St Johns House, begun in 1974 as the first of three similar blocks intended for the site, was faced in a dark brown brick with tinted windows. Varying heights and splayed corners helped to give it a sculpted appearance. Elizabeth House, designed by John Middleton and built in 1976–77, was a then-pioneering attempt to bring people back to live in the city centre. It too was built in grey concrete but given texture and pattern by vertical, deeply-moulded concrete ribs.

Arnhem House, a cluster of columns of varying height stepping down to the former Church of St John the Divine.

Each column has a pyramidal red-tile roof and the brickwork has horizontal bands and decorative panels.

Arnhem House and its neighbour Peat House, built around the same time, are influenced by the postmodern movement that was moving away from modernist simplicity in the 1980s. Peat House, at five storeys high not really a tall building, is faced in a bright orange brick with white brick horizontal bands and blue anodized panels and window frames.

LEFT: *Peat House*
MIDDLE: *St Johns House, Albion Street*
RIGHT: *Arnhem House*

Haymarket Centre from Gallowtree Gate

Beginning in the 1960s, but becoming more challenging from the 1970s, the city centre came under increasing competition from out-of-town shopping and this prompted a renewal of the built fabric of the city centre. In the 1960s ambitious plans had been drawn up for the wholesale redevelopment of a large area around the Clock Tower.

The Haymarket Centre was on a smaller scale than these plans but when it opened in 1973, was something new to Leicester in containing a covered shopping area, car parking, restaurants, a roof garden and the Haymarket Theatre within a single large building complex. The intricate pattern provided by older buildings on the site was replaced by long horizontal bands of red brick and glazing with elevated decks fronting Humberstone Gate and the Clock Tower, tough red brick around the northern end containing the theatre, softer light brown brick at the corner of Humberstone Gate and Charles Street, and a big cornice of brown and white concrete panels facing the Clock Tower.[123]

The Four Winds Clock, Halford House, Charles Street, 1955-59

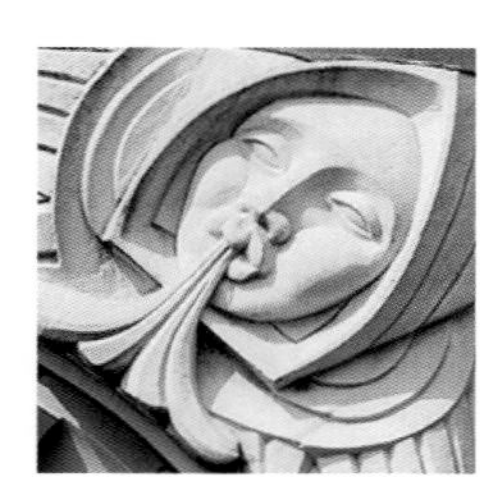

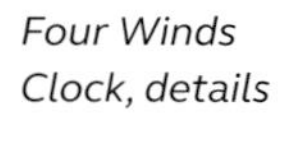

Four Winds Clock, details

Public art in Leicester had been fairly traditional or perhaps gently modern up to the 1970s. The surround to the Four Winds Clock, high above Charles Street on Halford House, was finely crafted in Portland stone in 1955-59 by Albert Pountney, former head of fine art at Leicester Polytechnic. The first abstract work in the city centre was Sculpture by Hubert Dalwood, a tree-like form in shiny stainless steel designed to complement the architectural lines of the Haymarket Centre. The work stands beside the stairs that led to the Haymarket Theatre and was once complemented by a living tree. The installation in 1974 produced a varied range of reactions from the Leicester media and public, and the city did not rush to add to its collection of abstract sculpture in the centre.[124]

HIGHCROSS
set
BOOTED
WORK
TO WEEKEND

FAR LEFT: *Entrance to Highcross with retained frontages on High Street*
LEFT: *St Martin's Square*

The next shopping redevelopment took inspiration from the complex street scenes of the medieval town. St Martin's Square was developed between 1982 and 1985, partly on the backs of former burgage plots and on a site once intended for a multi-storey car park. The development built in a deliberate way on the informal street layout and narrow frontages described in chapter 3. Small shops and cafes are grouped around a central space mixing materials like brick, slate, clay tile and render. A reused historic shopfront was salvaged from a demolished building in Market Place and a medieval timber building accomodated into a restaurant. Views unfold as the pedestrian passes through the arches from St Martin's and Silver Street and along the curve of the street connecting the square to Cank Street.[125]

The Shires, later incorporated into the larger Highcross (see chapter 24), was opened in 1991, introducing a mall running parallel to the High Street on the north side and retaining much of the Edwardian frontage to the street.

Multi-storey structures for car parking were built to cater for the growing demand for access by car to the city centre and to help to meet the challenge of competition from out-of-town shopping. In 1961 the Auto-magic car park proudly opened in Lee Circle. It was designed, by architects Fitzroy Robinson and Partners, to provide spaces for over 1,000 cars on a continuous oval ramp with a concrete parapet and also contained a supermarket, carwash and petrol filling station. Next to the site, on Wharf Street, was Britain's first and only drive-in post office.[126] Those facilities have gone but Lee Circle car park still looms, patched up, gaunt and massive, over the surrounding streets. Notions of architectural 'honesty' had changed by the time that Newarke Street Car Park was built by the city council in 1986–87. It was clad in brick to reflect its surroundings and has large openings in the manner of a factory or warehouse.

On the northern edge of the city, on the A6 at Red Hill, is a monument to the

Red Hill Service Station, former Mobil canopies, late 1960s

1960s motor age that offers a promise of the pleasures of the open road. The American industrial designer Eliot Noyes produced a standard design for Mobil in which the pump area was sheltered by tall, elegant, umbrella-like canopies intended to provide the approaching driver with a recognisable image for the company's petrol stations. The six listed canopies at Red Hill are thought to be the last surviving set in England of this design.[127]

Lee Circle Car Park

Humberstone Gate

High Street

Gallowtree Gate

Market Street

Gallowtree Gate was the first street in Leicester to be pedestrianised, at first shared by buses and people on foot, in 1971. Vehicles were excluded from Market Street in 1988.

Humberstone Gate and the Clock Tower became exclusive to pedestrians in 1996 and the High Street in 2007. Even the streets of the medieval town would have been filled by wagons and animals so the creation of a largely pedestrian centre, from King Street to St Peters Lane and the High Street to Charles Street, was a major historic change. It produced new street surfaces of brick and paving slabs to replace tarmac and new street furniture like the vertical coloured light columns in Gallowtree Gate and Market Street, all forming a stage for a more relaxed kind of city life.

Chapter twenty one

Knowledge

The various parts of what became De Montfort University were founded from the 1870s to serve the needs of Leicester's industry and commerce, and generations of the city's technicians, artists, professionals and business people have trained there. Much of the university's site was once occupied by factories and terraced houses.

The campus includes part of the Newarke where bitter fighting took place during the Siege of Leicester in 1645 (see chapter 5) and archaeologists have found evidence of Civil War defences during the university's building programmes. By reusing some of the city's most important historic buildings, the university has taken a stake in Leicester's built heritage.

The university's buildings came together over time in a pragmatic way. For much of the 1950s and 1960s the architecture of the colleges that combined to form Leicester Polytechnic in 1969 was utilitarian, resembling commercial architecture of the time. Some older factories, like the Queen Anne style Clephan Building on Oxford Street, were converted and reused. Modern additions,

De Montfort University, Hawthorn Building, details of bronze doors to extension

like the Fletcher Building, have now been radically altered and extended. In other ways, especially after the new university received its charter in 1992, the campus has gradually become more coherent. Traffic on Mill Lane has been calmed and a new public space has been developed (see chapter 25).

The Municipal School of Art was founded in 1870 and a technical school began in 1882. But the Hawthorn Building, built in 1896-97 to the design of Everard and Pick, is the earliest phase of development on the present campus. The style is a free adaptation of English architecture of the Tudor and Stuart periods and built in a rosy red brick with white limestone details. The big, imposing frontage to the Newarke was added in the 1930s. Percy Brown, then a lecturer at the Municipal School of Art, designed the bronze doors depicting the trades taught at the college and probably the Portland stone relief sculptures representing Venus and Adonis.

Kimberlin Library, right-hand red-brick section, left-hand grey tiled section

The first phase of the Kimberlin Library, opened in 1977, was designed for the polytechnic by Leicestershire County Council. The red engineering brick had become a popular choice of material even though it does not accurately reflect the softer orange-red brick of Victorian Leicester. The building had only narrow slit windows which lit internal spaces in which the main resources were books. The later phase, opened in 1997 and designed by Eva Jiricna Architects, was intended mainly for study using computers and has plenty of windows with external cladding in cool, grey ceramic tiles.

The Queens Building, designed for the School of Engineering and Manufacture by Peake Short and Partners and built in 1993, was based on the then-innovative principles of recycling heat generated inside the building from machines and human bodies, and of ventilating and heating the building as far as possible naturally. Construction in load-bearing brickwork, rather than using a steel or concrete frame, helped to provide thick walls to moderate the internal temperature. The main internal space is a 'street' which echoes the former layout of the site. Yellow, red and blue bricks make the interior spaces light and colourful. The external design is equally decorative with much use of pointed windows and cedar shingles and a skyline defined by a series of pointed gables and the tall stacks that draw air through the building.[128] The Queens Building was a radical design departure for the new university. Not everyone liked it at the time it was built and it still makes a singular contribution to Leicester's architectural character.

Queens Building, Mill Lane

Queens Building

Hugh Aston Building

The Hugh Aston Building is the most striking recent addition to the university's campus.[129] Completed in 2009, its scale steps down on the Oxford Street frontage to Magazine Gateway but its appearance is a strong contrast. Much of the building is clad in pale blue-green pre-patinated copper sheeting and the building has a series of large angled projecting windows facing Oxford Street.

The name 'Hugh Aston' roots the university in the deep history of the site. Aston was a 16th century musician and composer. He served as organist and choirmaster at the Church of the Annunciation which stood in the Newarke, a few metres from the building that now bears his name.

The foundation of a university college in Leicester followed many years of discussion. The former lunatic asylum close to Victoria Park, designed by William Parsons and a specialist asylum architect and built in 1837, had been a military hospital during the First World War. In 1919 Thomas Fielding Johnson donated the land for the foundation of the Leicester, Leicestershire and Rutland College. An explicit connection between the sacrifice of the war and the hope for a better future was embodied in the new college and still reflected in the motto of the University of Leicester: *ut vitam habeant* ("and they shall have life"). The land was open and development could proceed largely unimpeded by existing buildings.

Parsons's asylum, now the Fielding Johnson Building, became the college's first building and set the architectural tone for the early phases of development. The rather severely classical style and buff brick provided a theme for buildings on the site in the period of growth after the Second World War. Thomas Worthington and Sons of Manchester were commissioned as masterplanners in 1946.

University of Leicester, Fielding Johnson Building

Percy Gee Building

Not all of the masterplan was carried out but the Astley Clarke Building of 1951 and Percy Gee Building, built in 1958, continue the essentially classical theme although using modern components like steel windows. One of the best assets of the site is the lawn in front of the Fielding Johnson Building which is the setting of a piece from the university's fine collection of sculpture, the upright bronze Fronds of Souls made in 1990 by American sculptor Helaine Blumenfeld.[130]

The University College received its charter in 1957, becoming a university in its own right as the University of Leicester. This provided a new impetus for development and in 1957 Leslie Martin produced a plan for the land between Victoria Park and University Road which was developed as a small campus for mainly science departments. Martin's style was quietly modern, using long bands of dark-framed windows and a warm yellow brick, more colourful than the buff brick of the earlier phase of development but harmonising with it. Martin and Colin St John Wilson designed the Physics Building of 1961 and the delightful yellow-brick cube of the Rattray Lecture Theatre of 1962. The buildings enclose a paved rectangular piazza with now mature blocks of trees and shrubs which is the outstanding public space of its period in the city.

Leslie Martin recommended a complete change from his own calm and harmonious style for the next phase of development. At his suggestion James Stirling and James Gowan were brought in to design the building that would make their reputation and give Leicester an internationally recognised architectural landmark.

Rattray Lecture Theatre

ABOVE: *Charles Wilson Building* **RIGHT:** *Attenborough Tower*
FAR RIGHT: *The Engineering Building*

The Engineering Building was constructed between 1959 and 1963. Its complex geometry is dictated by the awkward shape of the site on the edge of the campus, by the functional requirements of the elements within it (offices, lecture theatres and laboratories), and by the need for a tower to provide a head of water for hydraulic experiments. The result is an arresting grouping of three-dimensional forms combined in a single building, with striking details like the gravity-defying raked floor of the lecture theatre on the south side and the crystalline glazed roof of the laboratory block. The main external materials are hard, red Accrington brick and red tiles. The Engineering Building was reglazed in the 1980s and the roof of the laboratory block was extensively overhauled in 2016. The Engineering Building is still as dynamic, intriguing and controversial as it was when it first appeared on the Leicester skyline over 50 years ago.

Two more towers followed. The university commissioned Denys Lasdun to design the Charles Wilson Building, sculptural in a square, blocky way and faced in grey concrete. The Attenborough Tower houses the College of Social Sciences, Arts and Humanities and is a relatively conventional tower with a regular pattern of office windows set on a base containing teaching rooms.

Attenborough Arts Centre

David Wilson Library

Just off the main campus, in Lancaster Road, the Attenborough Arts Centre is one of the city's best examples of a movement in which Leicester played a prominent part. The basic design principles allowing access to buildings for people with disabilities were established as long ago as 1909 and included in the design of the Guild for the Disabled in Colton Street (see chapter 15). In 1981, when John Dean was city planning officer, Leicester City Council appointed the first access officer in England, long before the introduction of a legal requirement for access to buildings under the Disability Discrimination Act of 1995. The Attenborough Arts Centre was designed by Ian Taylor of Bennetts Associates and opened in 1996. It was created for a wide range of users and incorporated measures to promote use by disabled people, all designed in a careful and discreet way within a light and welcoming building.

The university's building programme has continued into the 21st century. The Percy Gee Building has been altered and extended to include the O2 Academy,

David Wilson Library

where 1,400 music fans can enjoy their favourite bands. The 1974 David Wilson Library was remodelled and extended to a design by Associated Architects with a fully-glazed wall forming the front elevation. The same architects designed a Centre for Medicine on Regent Road to develop the university's research in medical sciences. The building has a row of vertical windows alternating with red terracotta cladding panels and a green wall, clad with climbing plants, on the western elevation. But it is the towers looming over Victoria Park, which can be seen from Oadby, Wigston and from as far as the M1, that ensure that the development and passing-on of knowledge give Leicester one of its most instantly recognisable landmarks.

University of Leicester, Centre for Medicine

Chapter twenty two

Change and adaptation

Population movement, arrival, settlement and the formation of new communities have been threads running through the 2,000 years of Leicester's history. Progressively since 1945 the city has become more diverse and Leicester people have business ties in over 50 countries across the world.[131] It is likely that Leicester has reached the point at which every citizen is a member of an ethnic minority: a historic landmark for the city and for Britain.

This diversity is reflected in the everyday life of the city and in celebrations like Caribbean Carnival, St George's Festival, Diwali, Christmas, Eid-al-Fitr, Vaisakhi, Hanukkah, Belgrave Mela and many more. But diversity also shapes Leicester's

LEFT: *Caribbean Carnival* **CENTRE :** *Diwali* **RIGHT:** *Vaisakhi*

architectural character and the development of areas with an atmosphere and appearance that reflect the cultures of groups who have settled there.

The impact of economic diversity in the city is demonstrated both by new buildings and by the adaptation of existing properties and historic urban areas. The reuse of factories like the former Imperial Typewriters works in East Park Road (see chapter 18) as small industrial units is an example of economic dynamism and the provision of a new use for a historic building. Green Lane Road nearby caters for a local Muslim and Sikh population with shops and cafés providing a number of alcohol-free places to meet and socialise.

In Belgrave Road and Melton Road–the Golden Mile–the significance of the area has changed over its history. This part of Belgrave was built over 30 years or so, beginning in the late 1860s, as an area of suburban growth in which rows of terraced streets (mixed with schools, churches, factories and workshops) were linked by the main road.[132]

The built fabric of the area has proved robust and adaptable to the needs of a mainly Hindu community. Some doorsteps, for example, are decorated with devotional symbols and front doors hung with garlands.

The main spine, Belgrave Road and Melton Road, forms a shopping street and a social and cultural hub for Leicester's South Asian communities and attracts visitors from far outside the city. The street scene is vivid and varied with painted brick frontages, some in groups of bright colours; displays of fruit, vegetables and household goods for sale; shop windows displaying sarees and ceremonial dress for men and posters for entertainers visiting from India or for satellite TV cricket.

The atmosphere is further heightened by savoury aromas from restaurants and snatches of music. The area does not quite have the teeming activity or the dense visual excitement of a street in an Indian city but there is a distant echo of the subcontinent.

Street scene in Belgrave Road

One of the best Art Deco facades in the city, built in brick, glass and faience, is the former Coliseum Cinema in Melton Road, built in 1933 and later called the Bollywood cinema and is now the Colosseum shopping mall and exhibition hall. Across Melton Road, the former Church of St Michael and All Angels, built in the 1880s, is the studio of the radio station Sabras Sound.[133]

RIGHT: *Former Coliseum and Bollywood cinema, Melton Road*

At the junction of Catherine Street and Weymouth Street, Shree Sanatan Mandir began life as the Carey Hall Baptist Church, named in honour of William Carey, a Leicester shoemaker, missionary and self-taught linguist who translated the Bible into 30 (mainly Indian) languages.[134] The hall became a Hindu temple and community centre in 1971 and more recently has acquired a cluster of *shikharas* (rising towers).

Further north, on Gypsy Lane, the BAPS Shri Swaminarayan Mandir is a meeting place for the community and stands at an important traffic junction. An industrial building was spectacularly converted in 2007 by the addition of an ornate porch, domes and *shikharas* in white reconstituted stone.

Masjid Umar, a mosque on Evington Lane, was built by the Muslim community in the Evington area in 2000 to the design of architects Kent Porter Warren. More recently, an additional community and education building has been added. The design of the mosque is confident and ambitious. It is built in buff brick and dark red polished granite with a gold-coloured dome and four minarets that provide a landmark in the suburban streets that converge on the site and an end-stop to eastward views along Evington Road.

ABOVE: *Shree Sanatan Mandir, converted to a Hindu temple and community centre*

LEFT: *Shree Sanatan Mandir, detail of decorative brickwork*

ABOVE: *Masjid Umar, Evington Drive / Evington Lane*

Masjid Umar, detail of dome and minaret

BAPS Shri Swaminarayan Mandir, Gypsy Lane

BAPS Shri Swaminarayan Mandir, external and internal decorative details

Architectural and decorative styles brought mainly from India and Pakistan, and features including domes, shikharas and minarets, have become integral to Leicester's skyline and street scenes. In time they will be seen as keys to the steady development of the city's architectural character, just as the architecture of churches is today.

The Sikh community has converted various types of building to community and religious use including a Queen Anne style former church in Clarendon Park Road and the former Gypsy Lane Hotel, a large brick pub built in about 1930. The Guru Tegh Bahadur Gurdwara in East Park Road retains its industrial appearance on the former main frontage but has a white onion dome and a grand entrance facing Rosebery Street, reflecting the Sikh religious architectural heritage.

Many of these conversions use modern materials like reconstituted stone and fibreglass. But the Jain Centre on Oxford Street, completed in 1988, goes a step further. The building was converted from a former Congregational church to a centre for Jains throughout Europe. The design, by an architect in India, added columns, arches and statues in marble, and other stones quarried and sculpted in India, in a design of great complexity and decorative quality, particularly inside the building.[135] The Jain Centre has become a familiar city landmark and a monument to the ambition and energy of the community who built it.

TOP LEFT: *Guru Tegh Bahadur Gurdwara, East Park Road / Rosebery Street*
LEFT: *Window detail*

Jame Masjid, Asfordby Street

ABOVE TOP: *Jame Masjid, dome and minaret*
ABOVE: *Jame Masjid, door handles*

Community buildings help to underpin the lives of many groups in Leicester. The Emerald Centre on Gypsy Lane is a focus for the life of the Irish community, established in Leicester since the middle of the 19th century.

The African Caribbean Centre in Maidstone Road and the nearby West Indian Senior Citizens Centre provide a similar focus for the city's African Caribbean community who have lived in the city since the 1950s.

Leicester's diversity can be expressed by areas in which one particular community is dominant or by the community and business activities of many groups in a single street. In recent years Narborough Road has become known nationally as one of the most diverse streets in England. This is based not so much on the presence of one particular community but on the wide range of businesses represented there, set up by and serving Turkish, African, Central Asian and Eastern European groups as well as more established communities already mentioned. The extraordinary variety of shop signs, posters and displays produces a street scene that reflects another dimension in the city's social and economic diversity.[136]

Jain Centre, Oxford Street

Emerald Centre, Gypsy Lane

African Caribbean Centre, Maidstone Road

Jain Centre, window detail

Jain Centre, Oxford Street

Abbey Park gatelodge

Abbey Park, refreshment rooms

Chapter twenty three

Green city

Leicester is a strikingly green city. From a high building, countryside is visible in almost all directions. Street views dominated by brick and tarmac often terminate in a vista of grass and trees. New Walk takes trees and green space into the heart of the city and public gardens and street trees provide shade and relief from brick and stone and help to absorb carbon dioxide.

After the provision of the recreation ground on Welford Road in 1839 (see chapter 8), it was over 40 years before the next public park was opened. The town council financed the laying out of Abbey Park, which formed part of a scheme for flood relief carried out in 1878. William Barron and Sons of Borrowash, Derbyshire were commissioned to prepare a formal design including lawns for recreation, formal flowerbeds, an American garden and ranges of greenhouses. Barrons's design also included a lake and sports pitches including an archery ground. William Barron was a nurseryman and a tree expert and 33,000 trees were planted in the park. James Tait designed a grand entrance in brown sandstone. The lodges are built in a mixture of timber framing with sandstone, brick and red clay roofing tiles. The style is based on English architecture of the 16th century with small touches of Gothic.

River Soar and the bridge linking the original part of Abbey Park with the later addition of the Abbey Grounds

The park was opened with great ceremony by the Prince and Princess of Wales on 29 May 1882. In 1925 the Abbey Grounds were added as a gift to the city, providing a more open area with its own atmosphere and a distinctive set of buildings by WK Bedingfield and Grundy that echo the style of Tait's lodges, but mixed with Bedingfield's 20th-century approach to Gothic (see chapter 9). The same architects carried out conservation works on the abbey ruins and Abbot Penny's Wall.

Abbey Park is a much-enjoyed public space and has over 500,000 visitors a year.[137] Its formal nature produces self-contained spaces that lend themselves to public art, a sensory garden, pets corner and a wildlife garden that attracts pollinating insects. The Chinese Friendship Garden, introduced in 1987 as part of a city twinning initiative, echoes the Victorian taste for exotic themed enclaves in public parks and private gardens.

The corporation bought land between Hinckley Road and Glenfield Road in 1897 and Western Park was developed in the early 20th century. The site was a fragment of the ancient Leicester Forest. Western Park still has a rural

Abbey Park, bandstand

Abbey Park, formal flower beds

atmosphere and contains a number of venerable trees including Old Major, a monumental oak close to the main drive from Hinckley Road. Native tree species and links to other spaces make the park an important habitat for birds and invertebrates and it is designated a Local Wildlife Site.

ABOVE AND BELOW: *Abbey Park, bridge to the Chinese Friendship Garden*

River Soar and tower of National Space Centre

The River Soar is fundamental to Leicester's history. Chapter 1 showed that the city began as a settlement by a river crossing and Leicester's name is probably derived from *ceaster*, a fortified settlement, by the River Legor, an early name for the river.[138]

Leicester's riverside is enjoyed by thousands of people yet remains a world parallel to the busy city. The eight-mile long park contains the city sections of the River Soar on its various courses, the Grand Union Canal and the River Biam. It has a diverse character: open and expansive in the north, urban and full of clues to the city's history in the section closest to the city centre. In the south the canal is enclosed by crack willow and black poplar trees with houses and factories pushing through to the water's edge: this is the classic edgeland; neither urban nor rural but with a quality of its own. The riverside is a place for recreation and movement but it is also a rich and complex natural environment with a varied ecology including plants, insects, birds and mammals and fish.

Mill Lane Bridge

Watermead Way Bridge

Until 1794, Leicester was the largest town in England not connected to the growing canal network, but in that year the River Soar navigation was extended from Loughborough, to the great benefit of Leicester's economy. Plans to extend the canal further southward were slow to be carried out but a link to London via Foxton and Norton Junction was eventually opened, in 1814.[139] The engineering of the river and the new canal leaves a complex legacy. One aspect of this is a system of bridges, locks, weirs, mileposts, signs, canalside buildings and distinctive canal-engineering features, like the narrow path under the low arch of North Bridge. Another is the array of the rugged industrial colours and textures of canal materials: blue and red brick, sandstone, granite, cast iron and timber.

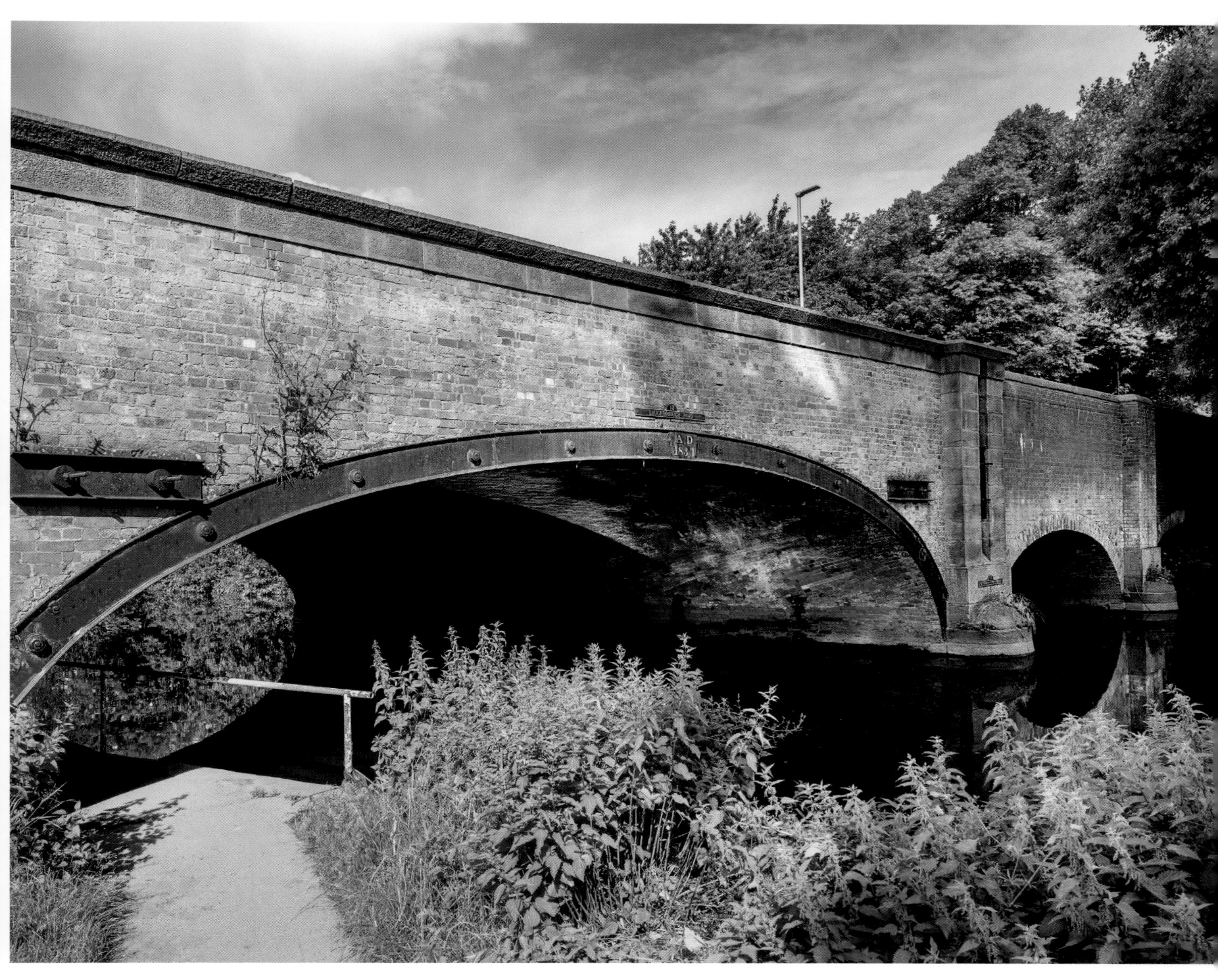

New Bridge, Loughborough Road

Bridges chart the city's history and growth. On the northern edge of the city, Watermead Way Bridge carries traffic over the broad river valley. Built in 1974, the innovative design was based on a hollow box beam which supports the road deck, the beam supported in turn by sturdy Y-shaped piers.

William Parsons worked for a time with the great engineer Thomas Telford and, back in Leicester in 1834, designed New Bridge carrying Loughborough Road over the river as an alternative route to the 15th-century Belgrave Bridge nearby. New Bridge is a low, elegant structure built in pinkish-red brick, sandstone and iron with bricks laid in a striking skewed pattern on the underside of the main arch.

Newarke Bridge

Between Soar Lane and the Newarke, the river marks the western boundary of the Roman and medieval town. West Bridge, historically the city's most important nodal point, replaced a medieval bridge which lasted into the 19th century. The present bridge, with the Leicester cinquefoil cast into the iron faces and sculpted medieval heads on the sandstone piers, was built by John Butler and Co of Leeds in 1890 to the design of the borough engineer EG Mawbey. Leicestershire County Council built the concrete bridge on the north side in the 1970s to take eastbound traffic. The Nearby Bow Bridge crosses one of the old courses of the river and is steeped in folklore surrounding the death of Richard III.

The Newarke Bridge opened up a previously secluded area on the east side of the river. It was also designed by Mawbey and opened in 1898. The basic structure is built in concrete, faced in brown sandstone with battlements reflecting the proximity of the castle. To the south, the Mile Straight was re-engineered in 1889-90 as a canal and to reduce danger of flooding. Gimson and Company built bridges at Mill Lane and Upperton Road. Both have a road deck slung on girders supported by shallow arches. The brick and sandstone piers are topped by Athenian Towers of the Winds at Mill Lane and by obelisks at Upperton Road.[140]

West Bridge

Plaque marking the site of the supposed disposal of the remains of King Richard III

Bow Bridge, over the old course of the River Soar, 1862. The red rose of Lancaster is in the left hand panel, the arms of Richard III's Plantagenet family in the centre and the white rose of York on the right

Aylestone Packhorse Bridge, 15th century

South of St Mary's Mills, there are four little arched, red-brick bridges which date from the time of the construction of the canal in around 1800. The line of Marsden Lane Bridge continues from the brick bridge westwards over the narrow 15th century Packhorse Bridge, built to carry coal on horseback from Swannington. The 11 arches over the marshy course of the river are constructed in a mixture of stones, including Dane Hills sandstone and Charnwood granite, laid as roughly-coursed rubble. Just to the north, the braced ironwork bridge carries the Great Central Way over the canal. The recreational way, converted to public use by the city council from the late 1970s, was once the route of express trains to London.

Abbey Park and the engineering of the Mile Straight were intended partly to manage flooding by controlling flow and making areas to store flood water. Protecting local people from the effects of flooding was a concern throughout the 20th century.

Climate change will mean that flooding could be an increasing threat to homes, health and business in the coming years and further flood protection measures are likely to be necessary. In 1968 parts of the city twice suffered severe flooding. The programme of works designed to reduce flood risk included diverting storm water to areas of open space. Increasing the capacity of brooks by building deep, concrete-lined channels had a more obvious impact on the city's architectural character.[141]

The Mile Straight and housing development on part of the former Pex factory site

Aylestone Meadows

Hamilton, landscaped floodplain

In the 21st century, methods for dealing with flood risk include sustainable urban drainage (SUDS) in new developments. These methods allow water flow to be controlled and stored in areas that provide space for wildlife and local residents. At Hamilton, the urban extension in the north-east of the city, flood water from the Melton Brook is dispersed naturally through watercourses and swales, which together contribute to an attractive natural landscape setting for the housing area.[142] The Hamilton scheme has attracted wildlife and provides a link to the rural landscape nearby.[143]

Until the 1980s, the riverside was a

Hamilton, housing development

messy and rarely-visited part of Leicester. A programme of improvement at that time attracted international attention and progressively transformed the riverside into a 985-hectare park: a green ribbon running from north to south through the city. Land is set aside for grazing and for sport and there are natural woodlands, lakes, marshes and flood meadows. The city council led the programme of improvement at the time and much of the work was done by young people on job training programmes. Today the council manages the riverside in partnership with the statutory agencies and volunteers.

Bridges on the Great Central Way support long-lived communities of ferns that thrive on the lime mortar pointing. The hedges on the former railway, bridges, buildings and old trees can provide habitat for bats, and birds, and the invertebrates which they feed on.[144] In 1989 the city council published a pioneering Ecology Strategy which set out a comprehensive view of wildlife habitats in Leicester, along with policies for maintaining and strengthening them.[145] The strategy was a factor in the award to Leicester of the first Environment City title.

Work continues to support wildlife in the city by creating habitats like meadows, wetland and woods, and linking spaces in green networks. Preserving these areas from development also helps to protect properties from the risk of flooding. Urban parks are managed to provide havens for wildlife. Private gardens, which make up 20 per cent of the land area of the city, are vital resources

FAR LEFT: *Great Central Railway bridge over the River Soar, Aylestone*
LEFT: *Canal bridge at King's Lock*

RIGHT: *Canalside brickwork*
BELOW: *Great Central Railway bridge over the River Biam, 1899*

for nature. Important research was carried out in Leicester on the vast range of insect species that can be supported by domestic gardens.[146] The city council and its partners publish regular Biodiversity Action Plans and continue to develop green infrastructure networks to improve quality of life for the city's people and wildlife.

The green city is a complex mix of parks, gardens, waterways, built structures, woodlands, allotments, cemeteries and former industrial sites. It is important for maintaining biodiversity and adapting to climate change, for promoting health and well being, and for economic development. Beyond these material benefits, the green city provides everyday access to beauty and relaxation and opportunities to enjoy the interest and delight of encounters with wildlife.

Chapter twenty four

Millennium

Leicester is growing fast in the early 21st century and has an increasingly youthful population. Large-scale developments have been successful in the past but economics and planning policy have mainly produced a series of relatively small-scale changes, including the reuse and adaptation of buildings and historic areas of the city. Trends such as 'big-box' supermarkets, often in the suburbs, have continued. But the range of architectural forms and materials in Leicester has increased in ways that are beginning to come together as a distinctive contribution to the city's architectural character from the present century.

The National Space Centre was Leicester's millennium project. It brought together the University of

LEFT: *National Space Centre, Exploration Drive*
ABOVE: *Blue Streak Rocket in the Rocket Tower, National Space Centre*

Leicester (with its prowess in space science), the Millennium Commission, the city council and the private sector which developed the scheme in partnership. The site is next to Abbey Pumping Station (see chapter 13) and the main galleries of the space centre were built into the former storm water tanks, the parts above ground clad in corrugated steel and steel mesh. The building, designed by Grimshaw Architects, opened in 2001 and is Leicester's most distinctive building of the 21st century so far. The bulging, tapering, 42-metre high tower containing a collection of rockets, its freeform shape formed by pillows of silver ETFE plastic, is one of the most striking features of the city's skyline.[147]

Dock, Exploration Drive

Development has been attracted to a previously unpromising part of the city following the opening of the space centre. In 2013 the city council opened Dock, a centre for the incubation and growth of knowledge-based industries. Designed by Maber Architects, the form is clear and simple with materials including dark-brown brick, zinc cladding and timber.

For many Indian villages, the communal and spiritual focus is the peepul tree. Belgrave Baheno Womens Centre initiated the Peepul Centre in Orchardson Avenue, now run by the Ethnic Minority Foundation. A range of services for the local community were brought together in a building of neat simplicity, designed by Andrzej Blonski and opened in 2005. The colourful, spacious entrance atrium gives access to a 300-seat auditorium, a bar and restaurant, fitness rooms, business units and an IT suite.

Dock, interior atrium

Peepul Centre, Orchardson Avenue

Peepul Centre, internal atrium

Leicester Tigers Rugby Club, Caterpillar Stand

Until the 1960s three of Leicester's nationally-known sports clubs played within a small area south of the city centre. Leicestershire County Cricket Club once hosted some of the greatest names in the game on the electricity sports ground on Aylestone Road, against the backdrop of pylons and cooling towers. A well-kept pitch and white-painted pavilion remain.

Leicester Tigers rugby club have played at Welford Road since the club was founded in 1892. Consistently one of the most successful rugby union clubs in England, the Tigers began increasing the spectator capacity of their stadium by the construction of the Caterpillar Stand in 2009, to the design of the stadium architects AFL. The club has ambitious plans to expand spectator capacity to make it a major centre for the game. A new stand opened in 2016.

Leicester City Football Club moved the short distance from Filbert Street to King Power Stadium in 2002, then named Walkers Stadium. Designed by specialist architects Miller Partnership, the seating structure has a robust engineering quality added to a sleek, glazed building fronting the river and containing reception, hospitality and conference suites, all dominated by the team's dark blue. In May 2016, the stadium was the scene of the greatest moment in the history of Leicester City and one of the happiest occasions in the long story of the city of Leicester when the team clinched the Premiership title for the first time, prompting worldwide interest and a huge public celebration.

Leicester City Football Club, King Power Stadium

St Peter's Square

John Lewis store, Highcross

Highcross shopping centre was opened in 2008 and reflected a change in thinking about retail development since the opening of The Shires 17 years earlier, and now part of the more recent development. Highcross is designed to be a place in its own right rather than a self-contained, completely indoor space. Although privately owned, the spaces within the development are open to the weather and form new streets, extending the established structure and life of the city centre into an area of the medieval town that was formerly mainly industrial. Housing, a cinema and restaurants bring people into Highcross after shops have closed and paving and planting produce a crisply designed and lively social space.

The architects of The Shires, Chapman Taylor, produced a masterplan and designed part of Highcross but the overall scheme was a collaboration between several architects bringing variety and distinctiveness to the whole.[148] The housing and ground-floor commercial units are clad in red brick and terracotta, echoing a long-established Leicester theme. But the John Lewis store, confronting the busy traffic of Vaughan Way at the back, is faced in glass curtain walling with a design based on a historic textile pattern. The Showcase Cinema de Lux is a folded freeform shape clad in shiny silver metal sheet.

The new development included two historic buildings that had both faced uncertain futures. A Georgian house at 59 Highcross Street and the Grammar School (see chapter 5) were brought back into use as part of the scheme, provided with a new context and re-used as restaurants.

Showcase Cinema de Lux, Highcross

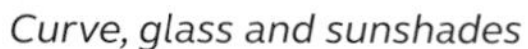

Curve, glass and sunshades

Curve, main auditorium

Autumn 2008 saw the opening of Curve, a new theatre for Leicester, and a programme of paving and lighting in the street around the new building. After many years of searching for a site, the partners in the project eventually settled on a difficult plot in the former industrial complex of Rutland Street, an area that was being given a new identity as the Cultural Quarter, providing an element of balance to the investment in Highcross. Rafael Viñoly, a Uruguayan architect based in the United States, was commissioned to tackle a complex brief. The big cliff of glass and sunshades towers over the street and reflects the buildings around it. Inside the circulation spaces around the two sophisticated auditoriums are lofty and dramatic and merge into the street scene outside through the sheer glass walls of the ground floor.

The LCB Depot in Rutland Street, a centre for Leicester's creative businesses, was the result of a radical remodelling of the former Leicester City Bus Depot, originally opened in 1969. White tiles were removed from the frontage and replaced by light-red brick with new windows. The former bus parking yard at the back contains a glass cube gallery and a six-storey, mainly glazed building containing additional units. Glazing is decorated with silkscreened images of plants and seeds by Linda Schwab. The architects, Ash Sakula, had designed a new theatre for Sparkenhoe Primary School in 2003, again partly by remodelling an older building. That building and the LCB Depot brought to the city what at the time seemed a fresh and original design approach.[149]

Courtyard elevation of The Depot, built 1969, converted anew as Leicester Creative Business (LCB) Depot, opened 2004

College Court, detail of internal staircase

College Hall, Knighton Road

Phoenix Square digital arts centre opened in autumn 2009 in Midland Street. The growing Cultural Quarter received further investment in 2015 when Leicester Print Workshop reopened in an unassuming factory unit in St George Street, built in the late 1970s for a steel fabrication company. The award-winning building was radically and imaginatively redesigned by Takero Shimazaki architects to become one of the best-equipped fine art print studios in the country.

College Hall in Knighton Road was designed by Trevor Dannatt and Leslie Martin in 1958-60 and was a student hall of residence for 45 years. In 2013 the buildings reopened as College Court, a hotel and conference centre. The existing buildings were all reused in the design by Associated Architects who also added a discreetly distinctive new reception building fronting Knighton Road. The buff brick with exposed concrete inside and out and the carefully designed spaces, along with details like fireplaces, parquet floors and a splendid spiral staircase, all provide what is promoted and seen by customers as modern period style.

Phoenix Square

NO ENTRY
Litter

Gateway College, Colin Grundy Drive

Liberty building and replica Statue of Liberty

CODE, Western Road

The years since 2000 have seen the rebuilding of many of Leicester's secondary schools, some under the then government's Building Schools for the Future programme, making a significant improvement in the environment of the city's schools for students and staff. Gateway College moved from the city centre (see chapter 25) to Colin Grundy Drive at Hamilton in 2009, a radical change in location and architecture. The design of the new school by Nightingale Architects is based on a glazed atrium running through the school with rooms for teaching accessed through this central space. The teaching rooms are clad on the outside in brightly coloured render and the tall glazed entrance is clasped by two bright yellow, curved sidewalls, all giving the school a youthful and welcoming appearance.

In Leicester today, 30 per cent of households have just one person and the 21st century has seen a growth in the market for housing for single people and students.[150] The architectural response to these trends has been mixed, but has produced some positive contributions to the city's architectural character. Summit, next to Upperton Road Bridge, was opened in 2012. Designed by Maber architects, it is a 66-metre high tower clad in dark-grey aluminium panels with a four-storey range finished in white and grey render, coloured panels and timber. The tower is easily the tallest building in the area but succeeds because of its elegant oval plan and the choice of a softly-reflective cladding material in a muted colour.

A series of residential conversions and new buildings in Western Road has changed a previously quiet part of the city. A notable example has been the conversion to CODE in 2012–13 of the former Equity Shoes factory, which was originally built in 1886, by the developer Jamie Lewis. The growth of a residential population in the area has helped to support a lively evening economy of bars, restaurants and pub theatre.

Summit, Upperton Road

Chapter twenty five

A sense of place

For centuries, Leicester was built mainly in materials made or quarried close to the place in which they were used. The particular colours of brick or stone, building forms and details dictated by the needs of particular local trades, the effect of climate and traditions of craftsmanship were passed on through generations. All these added to a pattern that was distinct to Leicester. That stability began to break down in the 19th century and today building materials are bought and sold in a global market so that, for example, a lot of the porphyry stone used in repaving in the city centre in recent years was imported from Italy.

Throughout its history, Leicester has broadly followed national fashions in building style, although it was sometimes behind the trend. During the 20th century building styles became national or international. But distinctiveness can be achieved by high architectural quality and especially by respect for history, context and urban structure and layout.

Buildings recognised as being of historic interest and value need not necessarily be centuries old, as this book has shown. But historic layout, areas and buildings reflect the steady growth of the city and are reliable keys to its distinctive character as a place. The historian Michael Wood has called the centre of Leicester "a great historic landscape" and much of the emphasis in planning and design since 2010 has been in stitching the elements of that landscape back together, particularly through the Connecting Leicester programme.[151] This has set out to re-establish connections that were lost in the planning of the decades after 1945. Inevitably some of the results have been compromises: traffic has to be kept moving and some of the less welcome legacies of the past cannot easily be put aside.

Belgrave Flyover, a structure that typified the traffic planning of the 1960s and 1970s, was demolished in 2014. There is still a big roundabout on the site but the community in Belgrave (see chapter 22) has been brought closer to the city centre in a way that would have been impossible when the huge concrete structure filled the view towards the centre and discouraged walking.

Belgrave Road roundabout and Belgrave Gate, after the removal of Belgrave Flyover in 2014

Fish and Meat Market

Magazine Square

De Montfort University's reshaping of its campus from 2004 included the creation of a new public space at the Newarke (see chapters 3 and 21), to give coherence to the northern part of the university site and to make a better transition between the university campus, the castle and the city centre. The L-shaped space (Magazine Square and Hawthorn Square) opened in 2011.[152] The squares provide a new setting for several key historic buildings alongside the new Hugh Aston Building, including the Georgian former Gateway School which is now used by the university. Another benefit has been to bring the Magazine Gateway into the space of the square after being marooned between busy roads for many years, accessible only through subways. The work was complemented by improving links with the city centre via Southgates and making more space for pedestrians and cyclists in Newarke Street. The new squares received their most distinguished visitor in 2012 when the Queen visited Leicester at the beginning of her Diamond Jubilee tour.

Perhaps the most ambitious project since 2010 has been the creation of a linked sequence of spaces through the medieval town, a route full of clues to Leicester's history. The demolition of the bulky red-brick Market Centre, which opened in 1973, has made way for a new public square on land probably built up for 500 years and has revealed views of buildings not experienced before. The market's Food Hall has been rehoused in a new glass and steel building, designed by specialist architects Greig and Stephenson, that opened in 2014. The new building abuts the Corn Exchange, bringing an outside wall into the interior, and has a sweeping curved side elevation following the historic shape of the Market Place.

Repaved streets link the new square in the Market Place to Cathedral Gardens, a calm, uncluttered space that provides a new setting for the cathedral.[153] Trees, full of blossom in season, shrubs and perennial plants, lawns and sculpture provide a calm place for visitors to rest and reflect on their experience of the cathedral and the King Richard III Visitor Centre.

The centre itself was designed by Maber architects over the site of the grave where the king's remains were found. It is a clean steel, glass and stone building over what was for many years a car park (see chapter 3). James Butler's bronze statue of King Richard, made in 1980 and originally sited in Castle Gardens, provides a tangible representation of the king's last moments at Bosworth battlefield.

Cathedral Gardens

Statue of King Richard III by James Butler, 1980, resited 2014

King Richard III Visitor Centre

King Richard III Visitor Centre, site of Richard's grave

High Cross, Jubilee Square

The narrow passage between the cathedral and the Guildhall leads to the third space in the sequence: Jubilee Square, laid out in 2014 on the site of a former public car park.[154] More open and dominated by stone than Cathedral Gardens, Jubilee Square gives the city centre a gathering place big enough to stage outdoor events, open-air cinema and the Christmas big wheel. It came into its own in the programme marking the reinterment of Richard III in March 2015, when Leicester people came together in a collective civic celebration. The stone column in the north-eastern corner of the square is all that remains of the 16th-century High Cross. After many years of being moved from one place to another, it is at last back within a few metres of its original site in the market place of Highcross Street.

Jubilee Square and the surrounding area take the story of Leicester back to its beginning. It is a modern space but built on many layers of Leicester's history. The site was part of the Roman forum. Close by are the Norman merchants cellar and the Guildhall and, to the east, the cathedral spire soars over the square. The enclosed precinct of the Norman Castle stands to the south-west. Until the 1950s, the site was bounded by medieval streets. Dating from the 15th century, Wygston's House, the oldest residential building in Leicester, stands on the south side. Even the inner ring road, defining the western edge of the square, tells part of a complex urban story. The long diagonal path across the square leads the eye to the city's oldest church: St Nicholas, with its fragments of Saxon masonry. Jewry Wall, the earliest surviving structure in Leicester, stands just beyond and a little further away is the site where, in the late Iron Age, the first people of Leicester settled beside the river crossing. This one place embodies the essential nature of a city with a profound and complex history: both a place in space and a drama in time.

Open-air cinema, Jubilee Square, summer 2015

Jubilee Square

Notes

INTRODUCTION

1. Patrick Geddes, *Civics: as Applied Sociology* (Hamburg: Tredition Classics, 1905) p. 10.

CHAPTER 1

2. Patrick Clay and Sarah Geeves, *Leicester before the Romans* (Leicestershire Museums, Art Galleries and Records Service, 1988) p. 21ff.
3. Matthew Morris, Richard Buckley and Mike Codd, *Visions of Ancient Leicester: Reconstructing Life in the Roman and Medieval Town from the Archaeology of Highcross Leicester Excavations* (Leicester: University of Leicester School of Archaeology and Ancient History, 2011) p. 9ff.
4. Historic England, The National Heritage List for England (Heritage List) entry 1013312.
5. The excavation was directed by Dame Kathleen Kenyon between 1936 and 1939.

CHAPTER 2

6. Morris et al, op. cit. p. 43.
7. Information from Nick Hill, Historic England.
8. Four-centred arch: a flattish pointed arch.
9. Vault: a ceiling or roof over a space formed by a combination of curved elements. Rib-vault: a vault with ribs expressing its form.
10. Crown glass: glass made by blowing molten glass into a bulb and opening out into a sheet and spinning while molten. Peter Swallow identified and dated the glass in the Magazine Gateway.
11. Alec Clifton-Taylor, *The Pattern of English Building* (London: Faber & Faber, 1972) p. 166.
12. Heritage List entry 1250274.

CHAPTER 3

13. CJ Billson, *Medieval Leicester* (Leicester: Edgar Backus, 1920) map facing p. 1.
14. Billson, Ibid. p. 26.
15. Limewash: porous applied outer coating for buildings made of mineral lime and water.
16. Diorite: a grey or dark grey igneous rock.
17. Cruck: symmetrical curved timber elements forming a rough triangle.
18. Paul Courtney, *The Archaeology of Leicester's Market Place* (Leicester: Leicester City Museums Service, new ed. 1998) p. 2. This reference forms the basis of much of this paragraph and those following.
19. Italianate: nineteenth century architectural style without columns influenced by the style of earlier large townhouses in Italy.
20. Van Heyningen and Hayward, http://www.vhh.co.uk/newspress/richard-iii-tomb-revealed

CHAPTER 4

21. Jack Simmons, *Leicester Past and Present. Vol. II: Modern City* (London: Eyre Methuen, 1974) p. 120.
22. Jeremy Crooks pointed this out.
23. Alabaster: soft and partly translucent type of gypsum often used in church fittings and monuments. Some types are common in the East Midlands and especially in the Trent valley. Humberstone alabaster was extracted from the later middle ages (Clifton-Taylor, op. cit. p. 190).
24. Y-tracery: intersecting stone bars in the form of a letter Y in a pointed surround characteristic of Early English Gothic.
25. WG Hoskins, *Leicestershire: An Illustrated Essay on the History of the Landscape* (London: Hodder & Stoughton, 1957) p. 103.

CHAPTER 5

26. The spelling of Wyggeston varies. The spelling used here is that used in Jill Bourne, *William Wyggeston and his World Leicester: Wyggeston's Hospital*, (2013) which has informed this chapter.
27. Staple: monopoly on the sale of wool granted by royal authority. Calais enjoyed this privilege from 1363 to 1558.
28. Founded by Robert le Bossu in 1143 (Heritage List entry 1012149).
29. Billson, op. cit. p. 95.
30. Heritage List entry 1012149.
31. Sir Charles Reed Peers, *Kirby Muxloe Castle Near Leicester* (Leicestershire Department of the Environment Official Handbook HMSO, 1983).
32. Billson, op. cit. illustrates a brick boundary wall to Greyfriars Priory, which he dates "circa 1500".
33. Richard Buckley supplied this information.
34. The plaque (mounted high on the wall of 1573 Bar & Grill, Highcross) lists 15 benefactors, recorded as having donated £69 5/- among them.
35. Bourne, op. cit. p. 36.
36. Colin Ellis, *History in Leicester* (Leicester: City of Leicester publicity department, 1948) pp. 66-7.
37. Siobhan Begley, *The Story of Leicester* (Stroud: The History Press, 2013) pp. 81-7.
38. John Nichols, *The History and Antiquities of the County of Leicester*, Volume I, Part 2 (Leicester: John Nichols, 1815) p. 620.

CHAPTER 6

39. Clifton-Taylor, op. cit. p. 210ff.
40. Header: the short end of a brick laid across the thickness of a wall. The long face of the brick is a "stretcher".
41. Norman and Underwood Ltd, <www.nandu.co.uk>
42. Leicester Museums, *Belgrave Hall guidebook* (1973)
43. Baluster: upright support for a rail in a balustrade or staircase.

44. Carrara marble: white or grey marble from Carrara in Tuscany, Italy. The marbles of Carrara are prized for fine sculpture.
45. The story of Edward Holdsworth and the memorial is told in Terry Cavanagh and Alison Yarrington, *Public Sculpture of Leicestershire and Rutland* (Liverpool: Liverpool University Press, 2000) pp. 187-8.
46. String course: horizontal band usually in contrasting material
47. Billson, op. cit. p. 183.
48. Pediment: flattish, often triangular gable sometimes used as a decorative device, for example over a doorway
49. Segmental: part of a circle that is less than a semicircle.
50. There are three basic Classical orders each with Greek and Roman forms. These are Doric, Ionic and Corinthian. They are fully explained in, for example: James Stevens Curl, *Dictionary of Architecture* (Oxford: Oxford University Press, 1999). The Doric is the first of the orders with simple rings forming the capital: the head of the column.
51. Fanlight: glazed window over a door.
52. Terry Y Cocks, "A Survival from Georgian Leicester: Number 17 Friar Lane" (*Leicestershire Historian*, No 42, 2006) p. 21ff.
53. Venetian window: three part window in which the central part has a semi-circular head; Diocletian window: semi-circular window divided into three openings by two vertical divisions; Rusticated stonework: stonework in which the joints are cut as recesses
54. Contemporary account in John and Thomas Spencer, *New Guide to the Town of Leicester … With … Illustrations* (London: British Library, Historical Print Editions, 2011).

CHAPTER 7

55. Susanna Watts, *A Walk through Leicester* (Leicester: T Combe, 1804).
56. Watts, Ibid., p130
57. Ashlar: smoothly dressed squared and finished blocks of stone. Whitaker suggests that the stone at City Rooms is Hollington sandstone.
58. Coade Stone: durable artificial stone made by the Coade company in London from 1769
59. Stucco: render made of lime and sand often containing cement from the 19th century
60. Graham Potts, "New Walk in the 19th Century Transactions of Leicestershire" (*Archaeological and Historical Society*, Vol XLIV, 1969) pp. 72-87.
61. Greek Key: square geometrical decoration making a continuous running ornament.
62. Pylon: ancient Egyptian structure with massive walls tapering upwards.
63. Enstasis: swelling in the middle of the length of a column to provide an appearance of strength and solidity.
64. Portico: covered porch, usually attached to a building, its roof supported by columns

CHAPTER 8

65. Billson, op. cit., p. 147.
66. Jack Simmons, *Introduction to A Walk through Leicester* (1967).
67. Jack Simmons, *Leicester Past and Present Volume II: Modern City*, p. 151.
68. Ned Newitt, *The Slums of Leicester* (Derby: Breedon Books, 2009) p. 8.
69. JD Bennett, *Leicestershire Architects 1700-1850* (Glenfield: Leicestershire County Council 2001) p. 25.
70. Pilaster: flat raised vertical strip attached to a building in imitation of a column. A giant pilaster rises through more than one storey.
71. Parsons's building accounts are deposited in the Leicester, Leicestershire and Rutland Records Office.
72. Included in South Highfields Conservation Area Character Statement (Leicester City Council 2003).
73. South Highfields Neighbours, *How Saxby Street Got its Name: World War One and the People of South Highfields* (Leicester: South Highfields Neighbours, 2015) pp. 39-48.
74. Malcolm Elliott, *Victorian Leicester* (Stroud: Phillimore Books, 1979) pp. 106-7.
75. Richard Gill, *The Book of Leicester* (Buckingham: Barracuda Books, 1985) p. 49.

CHAPTER 9

76. These issues are explored using primary material on the University of Leicester's Manufacturing Pasts website: http://www2.le.ac.uk/library/manufacturingpasts
77. Heritage List entry 1391809.
78. Art Nouveau: style of architecture, art and design established in Europe in the later 19th and early 20th centuries and characterised by flowing curved forms based on the human or plant forms.
79. Baroque: exuberant Classical style and 18th centuries revived in England in the later 19th century.
80. Atlantes (singular Atlas): male figures used as supporting column or bracket. The female equivalent is a Caryatid.
81. Cornice: projecting horizontal moulding.

CHAPTER 10

82. Quoins: stones or brickwork at an angle or corner of a building emphasising the corner. Rusticated: see note 55.
83. Drawings are deposited in the Leicestershire, Leicester and Rutland Records Office.
84. French pavilion roof: steep roof pitched on four sides often with a decorated ridge.
85. Post-modern: architectural style established in Britain from the 1970s that reacted against the orthodox modern movement and made free use of decoration and motifs derived from historic architecture and other sources.

86. Ionic: The second Classical order characterised by, among other features, column capitals with spiral projections known as volutes.

87. Kathryn Morrison, *English Shops and Shopping: An Architectural History* (New Haven CT and London: Yale University Press, 2003) p. 104.

CHAPTER 11

88. This and other information in this chapter is drawn from Derek Seaton, *Leicester's Town Hall: A Victorian Jewel* (Leicester: Leicester City Council, 2004).

89. Cavanagh and Yarrington, op. cit., pp. 157-65.

CHAPTER 13

90. Dan Cruikshank and Neil Burton, *Life in the Georgian City* (Viking London 1990) pp. 91-6.

91. Elliott, op. cit., pp71-73

92. Corinthian: the third Classical order in which the capitals have small scrolls volutes and are wrapped in leaves of the acanthus plant.

93. DE Roberts, *Leicester Gas Undertaking 1821-1921* (East Midlands Gas, 1978) pp. 91-6.

94. Porte-cochère: covered entrance structure to a building allowing access by vehicles.

CHAPTER 14

95. Geoff Brandwood and Martin Cherry, *Men of Property: the Goddards and Six Generations of Architecture* (Leicester: Leicestershire Museums Arts and Records Service, 1990) pp. 26-27.

96. Stephen Butt, *The History of Leicester in 100 People* (Stroud: Amberley Publishing, 2013) p. 51.

97. Arts and Crafts movement: artistic movement of the late 19th and early 20th centuries that sought to revive historic English crafts and decorative arts and to carry them into modern production.

98. A Stuart Gray, *Edwardian Architecture: A Biographical Dictionary* (London: Duckworth,1985) pp. 193-5.

99. Brandwood and Cherry, op. cit., pp 73-5.

100. Gill, op. cit., p. 51.

101 Shikhara: spire-like convex tower, a feature of Hindu religious architecture.

102 Catslide: roof of a single pitch covering more than one storey of a building.

103 Gill, op. cit., p. 50.

CHAPTER 15

104. Biographical information is drawn from *Leicester Town Trail: In Search of an Architect town trail* (Leicester: Leicester City Council, 1975) and Jean Farquhar, Arthur Wakerley 1862-1931 (Sedgebrook Press 1984).

105. Strapwork: decoration resembling leather straps crossed or interlaced deriving from Northern Europe but common in English architecture in the 16th and 17th centuries

106. Apse: recess projecting from the external wall, often semi-circular. A semi-circular chancel apse is characteristic of the French Gothic style.

107. Connie Crofts, *The Church of St Mark Belgrave Gate Leicester*, pamphlet published in 1950.

108. Heritage List entry 1074752.

CHAPTER 16

109. Seaton, op. cit., pp.36-37.

110. The words of the inscription on the north side of the memorial.

111. Inconnu (unknown) was the standard inscription used by the Belgian and French governments for unidentified soldiers. Elizabeth Blood of the University of Leicester supplied this information. The date of the death of "an unknown Belgian soldier" recorded on the nearby English Portland stone memorial is 30 October 1914.

112. Ordnance survey map 1931.

113. Information supplied by Katherine Wilson, De Montfort Hall.

CHAPTER 18

114. David Nash and David Reeder, *Leicester in the Twentieth Century* (Stroud: Sutton Publishing Ltd, 1993) p. 54.

115. Recollection of Toni Demidowicz, pupil 1962-69.

116. Curtain walling: outer surface of a building, often in glass or aluminium, hung on a frame and carrying only its own weight.

117. The architect of Stockholm Library was Gunnar Asplund. Arnos Grove Station was designed by Charles Holden.

118. For a number of years, Southfields Library was the base for Global Education Leicester-Shire, which held educational materials for local schools to help them teach on issues such as fair trade, climate change, diversity and interculturalism. This was relocated to Forest Lodge Education Centre in 2014, where it has been rebranded as the Global Learning Library.

119. Michael Taylor, "In Search of Vitrolite" (*Context*, No 65, March 2000).

CHAPTER 19

120. Information supplied by Mike Askey of Marsh Grochowski Architects.

CHAPTER 20

121. Hoskins, op. cit., p. 133.

122. Architects for the buildings in this group were: Post Office building: PO architects converted by David Robotham, Warwick; Elizabeth House: John Middleton, Leicester; St Johns House: Fletcher Ross and Hickling, Leeds; Arnhem House: Frederick Gibberd Coombes and Partners, London; Peat House: Douglas Marriott Worby Robinson, London.

123. WK Smigielski, *The Leicester Traffic Plan* (1964) p. 70 shows the elevated decks connected to a monorail.

124. Cavanagh and Yarrington, op. cit., pp. 119-120.

125. Architects were Nicol Thomas Viner Barnwell for developers Teesland.

126. John Minnis, *England's Motoring Heritage from the Air* (Swindon: English Heritage, 2014) p. 253.

127. Heritage List entry 1406858.

CHAPTER 21

128. Shingles: thin timber tiles.

129. Architects were CPMG of Nottingham.

130. Cavanagh and Yarrington, op. cit., pp. 171-2.

CHAPTER 22

131. Based on information supplied by Leicester City Council.

132. Christine Jordan, Leicester's suburbs: Belgrave and Western Park, an Architectural, Social and Economic History (unpublished dissertation 2011) pp. 18-19.

133. Architect: George Vialls of Ealing.

134. Architect: AE Sawday, opened 1897.

135. The History of the Jain Centre can be found at http://www.jaincentreleicester.com/about/our-history/

136. https://files.lsecities.net/files/2015/12/SuperDiverseStreets_Leicester.pdf

CHAPTER 23

137. Information supplied by David Mee, Leicester City Council.

138. This is not entirely clear but is based on the account in Barry Cox, *The Place Names of Leicestershire, Part One: The Borough of Leicester* (Nottingham: The English Place Name Society, 1998) pp. 2-3.

139. Jack Simmons, *Leicester Past and Present: Volume I: The Ancient Borough to 1860* (London: Eyre Methuen, 1974) pp. 130-3.

140. Tower of the Winds: a building in Athens (of about 48 BCE) incorporating a weather vane and devices for measuring time.

141. City of Leicester, Report of the Flooding (Special) Committee 25 February 1969, supplied by Brian Raper.

142. Swale: moist or marshy tract of land either natural or created for controlling water flow

143. Information supplied by Leicester City Council.

144. Sue Timms, "Caring for our other urban populations" (Context, No. 73, March 2002) and observations by Jeremy Crooks.

145. Leicester City Council Ecology Strategy (1989).

146. Jennifer Owen, *Wildlife of a Garden: A Thirty-year Study* (London: Royal Horticultural Society, 2014) p. 47.

CHAPTER 24

147. http://grimshaw-architects.com/project/the-national-space-centre/

148. Restaurants and offices with housing above by Glenn Howells Architects of Birmingham; 59 Highcross Street and the Old Grammar School by RG+P Architects and the John Lewis Store and Showcase Cinema by Foreign Office Architects of London.

149. http://ashsak.com/lcb-depot-leicester/

150. Information from 2011 Census.

CHAPTER 25

151. Michael Wood, from a lecture at the Guildhall, July 2015. Author's own notes.

152. Designed by Gillespies.

153. Designed by Gillespies.

154. Jubilee Square designed by LDA Design.

Index